Love
Is the Answer.

What Is the
Question?

Selected Writings and Talks
2016 - 2018

Cynthia Bourgeault

Cover photo courtesy of Brie Stoner

To all of my Wisdom students
—past, present, and future—
whose collective passion, brilliance, and love
have brought this collection into being.

And in a particular way to
our present Northeast Wisdom board
who encapsulate these qualities like light
pouring through a magnifying glass.

…and to Johnny, dear fellow wanderer, for sharing
your Zoi and your heart

~Cynthia Bourgeault

CONTENTS

Teilhard for Troubled Times

Abortion and the Greater Life

ACKNOWLEDGMENTS

Many thanks to all who collaborated in seeing this collection to fruition.

The idea originated at a Northeast Wisdom board meeting, though it had been germinating for a little while. Appreciations are due to my fellow members of the Northeast Wisdom Board of Directors for their support of the project in many ways: president Bill Redfield, Cynthia Bourgeault, Guthrie Sayen, Marcella Kraybill-Greggo, Matthew Wright, Mary Ellen Jernigan, and outgoing member Patricia Speak. The three M's, Mary Ellen, Marcella and Matthew, and Guthrie, offered their expertise and suggestions to the manuscript as well as moral support. Bill authored the Foreword with his generous presence. Cynthia and Mary Ellen were a tremendous help with the nuts and bolts of making a book, responding with immediacy and enthusiasm to every query.

Bob Sabath, long-time Wisdom teacher and organizer through Friends of Silence and in collaboration with the Claymont Society, gave great guidance and was always available for hours of assistance and moral support.

Holly Hough, the manager of the Northeast Wisdom website continues to lend a hand whenever asked, quickly, efficiently and with a creative hand.

Illia Delio of the Omega Center website, and dear friend and collaborator in all things Teilhardian with Cynthia, gave her generous permission to re-print "Love is the Answer. What is the Question?" and the three-part blog series *Teilhard for Troubled Times* originally published at omegacenter.info. The piece entitled "Christian Nonduality—*Seriously?*" was first seen on Mind Body Spirit (a publication of watkinsbooks.com) and a later version can be found at kosmosjournal.org as well.

Nicholas Vesey, of Aspen Chapel, and Laurel Catto of the Aspen Wisdom School, whose love and willing permission to transcribe the "New Year's Day Homily" in this collection, was helpful and up-lifting. This talk is available for viewing online at Aspen Chapel: Video Wall. The talk, "The Heart of Compassion: Exploring the Interior Landscape" was delivered at the 22nd Annual Festival of Faiths in Louisville, Kentucky in Thomas Merton Country and is available online. Transcribing both talks was a joy.

Cynthia's own books, particularly *Love is Stronger Than Death* and *Wisdom Way of Knowing*, contributed greatly to the "About Cynthia" page. Cynthia has been more than generous sharing her life story in a variety of settings, and brings that personal experience to her teaching on retreat. A number of interviews and articles accessible on the web are good references for her story, including her 2017 interview with Rick Archer at BuddhaAtTheGasPump. See the "Additional Books and Resources" by Cynthia Bourgeault for more information.

And finally, to Ken Davis, Joan Fothergill, Rebecca Parker, Kerstin Lipke and the greater family and friends of this particular Wisdom lineage, without whose love and interest, this little book would never have come into being.

~Laura Ruth
Collection Editor

FOREWORD

Whether she is unpacking a particularly dense section of one of the works of Teilhard de Chardin or Raimon Panikar, or whether she is reflecting on the implications of an academic Jesuit publication, Cynthia Bourgeault exhibits remarkable skills in helping the rest of us glimpse what she sees and understands. Utilizing a finely honed intellectual capacity and what is very likely a photographic memory, Cynthia is able to synthesize a vast amount of diverse material and distill it to its essence. For her students and her readers, this has been an inestimable boon and blessing.

Also, recently exemplified in the included series of writings on the abortion issue, Cynthia exhibits the capacity to articulate a cogent and coherent argument from its beginning to its conclusion. Stepping gingerly over restricted hallowed ground and at the same time drawing from hidden esoteric wells, she brilliantly and methodically states her case and makes new openings of understanding possible.

Hopefully this seven-part series will instigate a new and more enlightened national conversation around a previously impacted issue.

But in my estimation her greatest gift rests in her capacity to venture into the mystical truths of the divine–and then, drawing them in, she dares to express them in words, as she does in many of the writings in this collection. All of these faculties, particularly this last, are what makes Cynthia a gifted contemporary Wisdom teacher.

And yet, while these capacities help us to see the "what" of Cynthia's important lifework, they do not necessarily reveal the "how." To understand this "how" is to appreciate the ways in which the means of her teaching and her work coherently match the ends. Cynthia loves and, at the same time, empowers her students. She is not interested in being admired or adored (though she certainly is). Rather, her teaching and her writing is her conscious work, and she lives primarily to both share and activate what comes through her heart. Besides in her writing, Cynthia accomplishes this through her students. But more than desiring us to march lockstep behind her, she is much more interested in empowering our own work in the world. Indeed, in response to previewing the first draft of one my own writings, Cynthia encouraged me not to shy away from going "cheek-to-cheek with me directly..." Her teaching, then, is always generative and generous and always deeply collaborative. She trusts her students and depends on them to help form a conducive container within which Wisdom may emerge. To be her "student," then, is to also be her "collaborator" and "colleague."

These recent writings by Cynthia represent the depth of her Wisdom teaching as it is applied to the times in which we are currently living. Stretching from the autumn of 2016, just prior to the US Presidential election, through early 2018, they touch what is deepest on our own hearts and minds. Ponder them carefully and see where they lead you. Then act.

~Bill Redfield
October 10, 2017
Portsmouth, New Hampshire

LOVE IS THE ANSWER.
WHAT IS THE QUESTION?

"I was a hidden treasure and I longed to be known. And so I created the world, both visible and invisible."

This famous saying from the Hadith Qudsi, the extra-koranic sayings of Islam, speaks to the question of why God would want to bring creation into existence in the first place. Astonishingly, the reason given is not for majesty or dominion, but for *intimacy*, the yearning for self-disclosure, to know and be known. Seeded into the cosmos is that same primordial yearning, reverberating as a psychic harmonic of the big bang.

Teilhard de Chardin probably never encountered this quote. His familiarity with Islam was painfully limited, particularly in its mystical and Sufi branches with which he was ironically so deeply in tune. But in a real sense, this little gem of Islamic wisdom almost perfectly encapsulates Teilhard's own magisterial understanding of cosmic love, transparency, and

1

the personal.

How did we get to be here? How did *anything* get to be here? Teilhard judiciously sidesteps the classic metaphysical stipulation of a fall, an "involution" into matter. As a scientist rather than a metaphysician, he does not have to begin with the grand "why" of things; the "what" of them will suffice. And what he *actually observes* seeded into the stuff of the universe is a paradoxical dialectic: intense atomicity, granulation, the myriad bits and pieces of our materiality—and yet, at the same time, an underlying unity, and a force calling the "unorganized multitude" to move in the direction of "the unified multiple."(*Human Phenomenon*, 28) However the pieces may have gotten broken in the first place, what he observes everywhere in the universe is a countering force—he names it *love*—moving beneath the pixilated surface drawing all things together. "Driven by the force of love," he writes, "the fragments of the universe [continuously] seek each other so that the world may come into being."

For Teilhard, love is not first and foremost a sentiment, let alone a *sentimentality*. It is first and foremost a *geophysical force*, built into the very structure of the cosmos. In an astonishing one-liner toward the end of *The Human Phenomenon* he writes:

> *In all its nuances, love is nothing more or less than the direct or indirect trace marked in the heart of*

the element by the psychic convergence of the uni-
verse upon itself. (188)

In other words, if you're familiar with his theo-
ries of complexification and convergence, he's saying that this primordial impulse toward unification
(experienced at the biophysical level as *attraction,* and
at the psychic as *eros*) actually has its antecedent in
the physical shape of our planet itself, its perfect
sphericity inherently designed to shove things closer
and closer together so that they converge, complexi-
fy, and grow more conscious. Whether by chance,
"intelligent design," or its own innate teleology, the
whole thing seems to be set up like a cosmic grist-
mill for the extraction of consciousness.

When we love—when our own hearts reach out
in tenderness, desire, or plain old physical attraction—Teilhard asks us to remember that the cosmos, too, passed this way, seeking at the macro level
what we now experience at the micro. We are in
each another holographically, this world and us: the
whole of the "universe story" carved in our own
hearts, and the whole of our own story reverberating
with the cosmic heart.

Like that great other cosmological visionary Jacob Boehme (1585-1624), Teilhard has a penchant
for moving back and forth very quickly between the
physical and psychic realms. What for Boehme is
friction at a physical level very quickly becomes *an-*

guish at an emotional level; hence he can speak of the anguish of creation awakening to itself. In a similar way Teilhard moves between the "outside" of things and their "inside." From the outside perspective, love is a form of energy. It is an aspect—no doubt the *primary* aspect—of what he calls *radial energy*, the energy of evolution, the energy released in the process of complexification/consciousness. It is the force that runs through the cosmos as an energetic countercurrent to the Second Law of Thermodynamics, drawing things to become more unified, vitalized, and whole. From the inside—the psychic perspective—love retains its traditional meanings of compassion, intimacy, and generativity, drawing things to become more deeply themselves—"I am, may you be also," as Beatrice Bruteau concisely summarizes it. But it also conveys for Teilhard an additional connotation: *spiritualization*, which means the release of yet another quantum packet of that sum total of consciousness and conscience (and in French they are the same word!) seeded into the cosmos in that initial eclosion of divine yearning that launched the whole journey in the first place.

When Teilhard speaks of "harnessing the energy of love," he is speaking in both senses, both inside and outside. In the end, they are holographically embedded in one another, so the bridge between the cosmic processes and our own hearts is trustworthy.

Thus, we can look to our own hearts to tell us

more about what Teilhard sees as the essence of the complexification/consciousness process—hence of evolution (and hence, of love): his insistence that "*union differentiates*." We often think of love in terms of merging, uniting, becoming one, but Teilhard was wary of such definitions; his practiced eye as an evolutionist taught him something quite different. True union—the ultimate *chef d'oeuvre* of love—doesn't turn its respective participants into a blob, a drop dissolving in the ocean. Rather, it presses them mightily to become more and more themselves: to discover, trust, and fully inhabit their own depths. As these depths open, so does their capacity to love, to give-and-receive of themselves over the entire range of their actualized personhood.

The term "codependency" was not yet current in Teilhard's day, but he already had the gist of it intuitively. He knew that love is not well served by collapsing into one another. It is better served by standing one's own ground within a flexible unity so that more, deeper, richer, facets of personhood can glow forth in "a paroxysm of harmonized complexity" (HP, 184.)

The poet Rilke, Teilhard's contemporary and in many respects kindred spirit, is on exactly the same wavelength. He asks in his *Letters to a Young Poet*:

> *For what would be a union of two people who are unclarified, unfinished, and still incoherent? Love*

is a high inducement for the individual to ripen, to become something in himself, to become world, *to become world in himself for the sake of another.*

"To become world in oneself for the sake of another…" *Hmmmm.* Does love really ask us to become *world?* Does love make worlds? Is that what love does?

True, Teilhard does not directly tackle the question of first causes. But a clue to the cosmological riddle is surely embedded in his understanding of love as the driveshaft of evolution. Suppose this love is not a pre-existent "property" attributable to God, as in the classic substance theology of the past. Suppose it is instead an *alchemical process*: a tender and vulnerable journey of self-disclosure, risk, intimacy, yearning, and generativity whose ley lines are carved into the planet itself. The whole universe story has come into being because God is a hidden treasure who longs to be known. And the way—the *only* way—this knowing can be released is in the dance of unity-in-differentiation which is the native language of love. If it takes a whole village to raise a child, it takes a whole cosmos to bear forth the depths of divine love.

~*September 12, 2016*
The Omega Center at omegacenter.info

LINES OF MY OWN COMPOSED ABOVE TINTERN ABBEY

We'd arranged to spend a day of sightseeing on my most recent teaching swing through the UK, so the afternoon of November 7, 2016, found me in a car with my host Jackie Evans and my old friend John Moss, winding our way back to Bristol after a magical day of exploring some fabled holy sites and "thin places" in the picturesque Welsh countryside.

Darkness drops quickly in November; the sun was already barely cresting the ridgeline when we rounded a bend in the Wye River, and suddenly there was Tintern Abbey.

The sight does, literally take your breath away. There, nestled in the riverbed like a strange Gothic botanical, more growing *out* of the landscape than towering over it, stand the haunting ruins of a 12th century Cistercian Monastery, still largely intact. In 1536, it fell victim to Henry VIII's Dissolution of the Monasteries edict, his brutal initiative to disestablish the Roman Catholic Church in England.

Monks were deposed or slaughtered, the building was sacked and vandalized, its treasures were confiscated for the crown. Three centuries of peaceful and compassionate striving in this "school for the Lord's service" ended in an orgy of violence.

Over the centuries, the old stonewalls fell deeper into decay. Vines and wild brambles began to claw at their sides. The Romantic poets and painters loved it. By the time the poet Wordsworth visited the place in the early nineteenth century, it far more resembled a Druidic temple or a wildly surrealistic set for a Dionysian mystery cult than any kind of sober and lucid monastery, let alone a Christian one.

Once inside its walls, however, I recognized the vibration instantly. I've been to other such Cistercian sites—Fontenay in Burgundy, The College des Bernadins on the Parisian Left Bank. I've also prayed with the monks at the beautiful Abbey of Our Lady of The Holy Spirit in Conyers, Georgia, modeled closely on these ancient, architecturally stunning Cistercian sites. The energy is palpable, serene—distinctly feminine, unmistakably Cistercian. Funny, I had forgotten—or perhaps never realized—that Tintern Abbey was a Cistercian house...

The day was unusually cold for early November––fortunately, as it turns out, for us, for as the sun swiftly disappeared beneath the ridgeline, the few remaining tourists disappeared almost as swiftly. John and Jackie and I were soon all alone in this great, solemn sanctuary, its roof wide open to the darkening sky, its former stone floors now a carpet of green.

I found myself being drawn more and more insistently to the east end, where a gaping window and a small outline of stones marked off what would once have been the steps to the high altar. And as I allowed myself to be drawn, those words from T.S. Eliot's Four Quartets began to gather in my mind:

> *You are not here to verify, instruct yourself, or inform curiosity. Or carry report. You are here to kneel. Where prayer has been valid...*

And suddenly I indeed found myself kneeling before that imaginal altar railing, and then in full prostration. The energy of it literally pulled me down. And there, on the eve of the American presidential elections, those ancient stones again began to speak, and in a few timeless moments some of their own ancient knowing came to be planted within me.

Words (even "reflected in tranquility") cannot begin to convey it, since like most of those brief downloads mediated through what Gurdjieff called "higher emotional center," the vibrational intensity overwhelms the rational faculties and leaves one stammering in the dust. It's happened once or twice before, always like this.

Let it be said that when I rose to my feet once

again, I already knew beyond any doubt what the election results would be, and where the wheel set in motion the following day would most likely lead. My heart ached, but I was at last ready to face it.

It was not the *content* of the message but its emotional coloration that left me so transfixed. With infinite tenderness, resolve—like the eyes of Michelangelo's Pieta I had seen for the first time only weeks before at the Vatican—it spoke to me in those moments, shared what could be shared of the quiet endurance in the face of reversal, deepest sorrow, human atrocity. "Yes," said the walls, quietly, "we know... And yet, through all of this, something still stands."

"Just as we are still standing now," they whispered to my heart:

> —*and see how we have drawn you here and you are listening right now. Do not look upon us as a destroyed monastery, but as a living transmission.*
>
> *Know that what is forged in the alchemy of love is beyond the of ravages of time. All else may dissolve; this alone remains. But in your own transfigured heart, you will always find it.*

Then the walls fell silent, and the intensity slowly waned. I rose, rubbed the mud off my pants, and rejoined my friends. As we traced our way back to

the car, the last ray of sunset set the whole scene
aflame in a final eloquent coda.

> *Sin is behovely, but all shall be well, and all man-*
> *ner of thing shall be well." (Julian of Norwich)*

~November 11, 2016
Northeast Wisdom at northeastwisdom.org

NEW YEAR'S DAY HOMILY
ASPEN CHAPEL
JANUARY 1, 2017

Good morning all. I want to add my greetings, and give a special thank you for those who have made the effort to drag yourself out of bed on the day after New Year's Eve or, those who have come inside on a perfectly beautiful skiing day. I think there is a real importance in marking this transition; this New Year's Day—symbolically given to transition—of a year upcoming that we know is going to be heavy with transition. It is good to have this spiritual force gathered here and we *do* have some work to do together. Please don't think about what we are going to be doing today so much in terms of spiritual entertainment as in terms of gathering the energy of our hearts and our beings, to be a presence in this planet, a presence in the lineage and in the stream of the path of compassionate love that we stand for.

With that in mind, you are going to begin to notice, that if there is one theme that is running through the day, it is the theme of expansiveness or spaciousness. It is at this depth—in a greatly expanded universe—that we are going to find the hope, the strength, the reinforcement, and the courage to really lead and witness in a planet that *needs* spiritual presence.

We are going to be expanding our hearts and our minds, and even our geographical vista today. Two weeks ago, you may have heard the beautiful, traditional service of Lessons and Carols. The traditional formula is that the lessons tell the story of the history of the planet from Adam and Eve to the birth of Christ. Of course, as we know now, by the time we got around to the fall of Adam and Eve, the planet was roughly half way through its four and a half billion-year journey, as scientists calculate based on the energy still left in the sun. We were already half way through. What happened for the first two and a quarter billion years? How does this fit in our story?

I have long thought that we should have a first lesson in the Lessons and Carols that actually celebrates the beginning of our planet. That is what we are going to do to open the service today. The lesson comes from Teilhard de Chardin from his beautiful book *The Human Phenomenon* (37). The carol "Of the Father's Love Begotten," will pick up that sense of cosmic vastness.

Lesson One. Imagine yourselves back at King's College, Cambridge, and David Wilcox and the choristers are ready. The first of the lesson readers steps up and reads:

Some thousands of millions of years before this, not, it seems, through any regular process of stellar evolution, but as the result of some incredible chance; stars, brushing up against each other, rupture, from within. A fragment of matter formed of particularly stable atoms broke away from the surface of the sun. Without cutting the ties attaching it to the rest of things, and just to the right distance from the parent star to feel its radiation at moderate intensity, the fragment agglomerated, coiled in on itself, and took shape. One more star had just been born. This time, a planet. Imprisoning the human future within its globe and motion.

We'll sing:

Of the Father's love begotten
ere the worlds began to be,
He is Alpha and Omega;
He the source, the ending He,
of the things that are, that have been,
and that future years shall see
evermore and evermore! ...

14

"Evermore and evermore." That is, in fact, an old piece of Gregorian chant. It comes from the 12th century originally. One of the things which Nicholas Vesey, chaplain at Aspen Chapel since 2014, beautifully and helpfully introduced, was to begin the services with a time of meditation or spiritual preparation to get us here. It's a really good thing because to generate spiritual energy, you can't just do it with your mind. You have to bring your *whole* being here.

Today we are going to begin with a "being here" meditation, again working on the theme of spaciousness.

> *I invite you, first of all, to put your feet on the floor. Forget everything, except the fact that you are here. Let it go. You are here, present. Take a couple of deep breaths and let everything that isn't here simply fall off your shoulders like snow off the roof.*
>
> *Now, bring your attention to your feet. Usually they are the thing that we check at the hat rack when we come to worship. Press them down, against the floor, and let your attention fill them with sensation. Sometimes when you do that, they will actually tingle, alive with, "thank you, we're here too."*

Where are your feet practice

15

Feel them pressing down against the floor. Notice if using that same power of attention and sensation you can take them deeper. Five feet down, ten feet down, a thousand feet down. Until they finally connect with the rest of the granite of the planet, the geology of this valley. The place where all the mountains rise up from their bases. See if you can sense your way all the way down to that bedrock.

As those mountains begin to impact your feet, start to rise again by sensation, and feel the weight of those great mountainous beings pressing down upon the earth, feel the firmness, the solidity—the hereness. Then let yourself sense the vastness of the air, the sheer geological expanse of the space between those mountains, filling up this bowl of a valley.

Know that in that space, and still in the elements of those mountains, that air, are the primordial elements that exploded and agglomerated when our planet was formed. In that is the stardust, the residue of the big bang. And that stardust is in you. It is part of your physical frame. You are part of the legacy of fourteen billion years of the universe story, part of 4.5 billion years of the earth story. It lives in you as part of your physical being. You belong here. You are indigenous. You are a part of this story.

Let that vastness and the whole lineage in time and space anchor you, hold you, as I recite what's known in the tradition as the collect for purity:

Oh, Love Divine, to Whom all hearts are open, all desires known, and from whom no secrets are hidden, cleanse the thoughts of our hearts by the inspiration of your Holy Spirit that we may perfectly love you and worthily magnify your holy name in Christ our Lord. Amen.

collect for purity

See if you can hold on to that sensation in your feet, that sensation of vastness, as we read what is the traditional gospel for the first Sunday after Christmas. The magnificent cosmic words from the Gospel of John:

In the beginning was the Word, and the Word was with God and the Word was God. He was in the beginning with God. All things came into being through him. And without him not one thing came into being. What has come into being in him was life. And the life was the light of all people. The light shines in the darkness and the darkness did not overcome it.

There was a man sent from God, whose name was John. He came as a witness to testify to the light so that all might believe through him. He himself was

gospel of John

17

not the light, but he came to testify to the light. The true light, which enlightens everyone, was coming into the world.

He was in the world and the world came into being through him, yet the world did not know him. He came to what was his own and his own people did not accept him. But to all who received him, who believed in his name, he gave power to become children of God who were born not of blood or of the will of the flesh, or of the will of man, but of God.

And the Word became flesh and dwelled among us and we have seen his glory, the glory as of the father's only son. Full of grace and truth. From his fullness we have all received, grace upon grace. The Word of the Lord.

As you have noticed, I am playing the cosmic theme today. We are stretching our sense of time, in space, of the immense canopy that we are playing on. Stretching our senses as far as possible over the course of the whole fourteen billion-year history and scope of the universe story. I believe that it is from this perspective—and perhaps *only* from this perspective—that we can find what is most needed in our world as we enter this new year with deep hope and with an assurance that this hope is not in vain.

It is written into deep time—this hope—into deep space.

Some of you may know that the eve of election day this year, November 7, 2016, found me in the UK in the west of England where I had been doing a week of teaching. We had arranged for day of sightseeing, and took off to look at the thin places and holy spots in the Welsh countryside just north of Bristol. It was just about sunset as we came around a river bend in the wide valley and there, all of a sudden, was Tintern Abbey. Well, I had known about Tintern Abbey; everyone who took English Lit in high school knows about Tintern Abbey because Wordsworth wrote some lines above it, right? But I had never seen it before, and I knew nothing of the backstory.

I quickly discovered the backstory there. That it was a Cistercian monastery. That is the same order, basically, as our monks over the hill in Snowmass. It's a reform of the Benedictine Order. A place of strict silence and prayer and spiritual work. It was founded in the 12th century, did really awesome spiritual work for about four centuries, and then fell victim to Henry the VIII's Dissolution of the Monasteries Act in 1536. Cromwell's' band fell upon it, sacked the place, carried off some of the monks, murdered others, took off the roof and basically destroyed the outer structure. And there it stood.

Vines grew over it. Wordsworth found it as a sort of mystical, Gothic, druidic palace. When I got there, I was stunned. I looked at it, and when we came through the space I realized: I can still smell the Cistercian feeling here. There is a definite ambience. A feminine roundness and wisdom—a completeness. I could feel that, even after bitter destruction—there was something still *gathered* there. It began to draw me. It began to pull me. Until finally I found myself right at what would have been the foot of the high altar, five hundred years ago, still with the remains of an open window above me. The next thing I knew, I was on my knees, then on my face, and time disappeared. When I got up again and began to reconstruct what had happened, I knew with absolute certainty how the election was going to turn out. There was no doubt in my mind what was happening. But along with that came two very strong messages from these walls. The first one was:

This happens in the human story.

The fact that there is the good, the true, and the beautiful is no guarantee against periodic eruptions that take the whole thing down. This has happened over and over and over again in the human story. It is only *we* who have lived in a bubble for the past seventy years. Sadly—this happens. It is part of the human story. *Deal.*

*But look, something called you. Something re-
mains, the good, the true, the beautiful—work
that is done, the work of value, of spiritual openness—remains. It still has the power to reconfig-
ure, to call, to heal. To speak eloquently.*

It was with those two messages that I came back
to the States. I flew home on election day; and they
have basically framed my sense of what's happened
ever since. It is not my intention to talk politics today. Let's stay with sociology. It doesn't stray into
politics, however, to say that an outcome of this
election is that it represents a powerful rebuff of
what are so many of the liberal progressive value
system's sacred cows.

Inclusivity, multiculturalism, gender identity, eco-
logical sustainability, and radical, universal, compassion for the most poor and the most marginalized:
these seem to be under at least passive, if not active,
threat. To the extent that many of us stand for those
values and have been guided by those values, there
is a deep sense of grief and disorientation. "*What
happened? What do we do?*"

I find that many of my friends who have worked
in liberal social causes for years, are disoriented and
despairing. "*How* did this happen, what do we do
now? We are going to see the deconstruction of
'right'. Consciousness is taking a step backwards."

There is talk of the Kali Yuga, the time of darkness, and comparisons with Germany in the 1930's. I have to say, I think this is not helpful, in any way whatsoever. It creates what Valentin Tomberg calls in *Meditations on the Tarot*, an egregore. That is to be, a psychic entity that begins to gather force because people feed energy into it. If we feed energy into the image that this is a monstrous age, a dark age, a reversion to primitive upheavals, we are not only going to be unable to *help* what's happening in our time—we are going to be unable to *see* in a deeper way where the hope lies and what we must do.

What is needed, I think, is not fear and falling on our swords. Not laments, not grief, but deeper and broader vision. A kind of vison which unfortunately is not going to be easily accessible to the liberal intellectual establishment which has guided the talk in our time. It is a vison of a much more spiritual nature—a lot of which is only made possible by regular and faithful spiritual practice. Meditation, lectio divina, the Gurdjieff work, yoga, transformation— spiritual practice that opens up a different path of insight. From that perspective, a different window of opportunity begins to present itself.

One of the reasons that I have brought Teilhard de Chardin into this conversation today is because I believe that he offers us a model and a reservoir of deep hope. A perspective, that can allow us to come together and stand with joy and confidence. Teilhard, as many of you know, was a Jesuit priest, scientist, and mystic who lived in the first half of the century. He was famous—equally famous—as a paleontologist and as a Christian mystic. He is the first person to really paste a Christian mystical vision on a fourteen billion-year evolutionary canvas. And what is interesting about it, is that the proportions still fall correctly. It is a fascinating and hopeful journey.

Essentially, Teilhard sees the entire fourteen billion years of our universe story as, and I quote, *"a rising tide of consciousness carried on evolution."* In his take (to do this really simply), we start with atomized consciousness. Consciousness is seeded in the universe as a kind of fourth dimension, but it is all pulverized and isolated and separated so it doesn't have any force. Over the course of evolution things come together to form units. Elementary particles form atoms, atoms form molecules, out of the molecules and the polymer chains come cells. Cells carry life, and we have more and more complex plants and animal forms, until in human beings we see self-reflective consciousness. Evolution—aware of itself. Over fourteen billion years things have come together to form more powerful organic vehicles of consciousness that allow consciousness to manifest more and more brightly. It's never gone back.

In fact, at that time when the Adam and Eve story hits, in Teilhard's version, we have crossed a mid-

23

point—to a place where we are actively being drawn—through the Christic presence, to the fullest emergence of evolution as universal compassion and love. And what is really on our plates at the next stage, says Teilhard, is to form collectively the next organic body of humanity. A body based on our one organic oneness. As cells form a human being, we can manifest as a human race, with yet greater depths of compassion, consciousness, coherence, forbearance. We can truly show forth and bring forth what the heart of God is like—the hidden treasure that longed to be known—as the Sufi's said, and so it created the planets. That's Teilhard's vision; pretty helpful.

Interestingly, this is not Pollyanna. Teilhard's vision of the universal oneness of humankind first came to him in the trenches of World War I, surrounded by the carnage as he served as a stretcher bearer. It was after World War II when he was finally released from exile in Communist China to come home, with Europe still quivering in the wake of the holocaust and the atom bomb, that he pointed out that deep hope runs over deep time.

Teilhard says, evolution was chugging along for ten thousand years, we were right on the edge of giving birth to a whole new form of consciousness––and Ta Da! Ice Age! Ten thousand years later it picked itself up again and *immediately* after that we see human beings, forms arising that are using fire and making tools. There *is* a cosmic purposiveness, a cosmic intelligence, that is built in. That meets us. That carries us. If we do not hold too tightly and do not measure meaning in decades, or even centuries, we *can* find the current and flow with it.

That's the message that comes from Teilhard. Interestingly enough, some of you are already reading a paper that is circulating around from Ken Wilber. It is a ninety-page contribution on the election as seen from levels of consciousness. Ken Wilber's bottom line is that, very much like Teilhard, this is a correction. Seen from the levels of consciousness, what happened is that the leading edge of evolution got off track. What he calls in color code, "green," wandered in denialism and narcissism, and impacted political correctness, victim consciousness, and a kind of flunky egalitarianism that had to throw out all hierarchy because it couldn't see that some forms of organization were needed. "Green" became impacted.

Wilber sees the election as a rising up of a necessary corrective. Evolution will move on, consciousness has not been diminished. It's been readjusted, and we are going to be part of that readjustment in the next period, certainly in the next four to eight years. What this really means, beyond simply correcting the intellectual at its own level, is that the evolutionary movement and creation is going to pick up the thread where there is a real infusion, energy and vision from people that are beginning to move to the integral and nondual levels of consciousness. People who are already thinking and seeing from the basis of universal wholeness. I like to say that the difference in these levels is that Green says "co-exist" integral says "coalesce."

Let's form this body. Let's become one humanity, one planetary species. Let's learn how to do it. Let's organize our hearts and our souls so much from the inside that we can collectively bear forth a quality of beauty, goodness, power and strength that resembles the Heart of God and that profoundly honors consciousness in the next era. We can do this. What this means for people of good will and progressive values is to continue to do the work we are doing, with more conviction and more sense of universality. Continue with the meditating, with the spiritual practice, continue serenely to be planetary citizens, to fly the earth flag, to understand that we are coming into oneness, and to live out of that oneness and minister out of that oneness.

Our task is to stay the course. To be gentle. To be open. Above all, to do the work that you need to do personally in your own being to go deep in mystical practice. Because the hope coming up to meet us is no longer a kind of secular hope based on worldwide progress. It is a spiritual forming of a new container, to hold the face and the heart of divine love. That is holy work. That is work we can give ourselves to do that will have some bearing on the planet.

No work is wasted. We are receiving help, not only from the depth of the planetary history rising up like those mountains to hold us, but from the world of those gone beyond. The saints, the holy ones, those that watch over our planet. If we can keep a heart that is clear enough—pull them in—make a conveyor belt; our energy, even in small groups, will hold this planet on course as it goes through this necessary transition. These are my words of hope and my call to order in the New Year. Let's get working, let's get moving. Let's share the joy. Let's share the good news of our human beingness.

As we move into the last of the service, you are going to hear a wonderful carol called "Walking in the Air," with the words:

> *"We are walking in the air, we are floating in the sky so high." Imagine a sleigh ride with two lovers over the face of creation. Imagine yourself, as you listen to the music, looking out like Neil Armstrong at the beautiful blue earth, feeling the oneness, feeling the vastness, riding like Job when God gives him the tour of the wonders of it all. Allow this to carry you to that spaciousness again. Maybe as you look down you can even see Tintern Abbey.*

We are going to—as our last work together to-day—offer together Teilhard's Mass on the World. And this is a very interesting thing. I call it a negative space Eucharist, because it is done without bread and wine. The deal is that Teilhard, when he was a young man, was on an archeological expedition in the Mongolian deserts. As a newly-minted priest of the Catholic Church he was required to offer mass every day. But hey, there was no bread, there was no wine, there was certainly no sacred silverware, chalice and vessels. It occurred to him in a mystical inspiration to offer as his bread and wine the bread of human suffering, or the bread of human toil and labor, conscious labor, and the wine of human suffering. He did this as an offering on behalf of and in solidarity with all humankind.

On this first day of the year in 2017, in the deserts of Aspen, Colorado, we will offer this *Mass on the World*. You will have a part in it too—as we offer this completely holy, non-hierarchical, mass on the world.

~*January 1, 2017*
Aspen Chapel, Aspen, CO.

KEN WILBER'S: TRUMP AND A POST-TRUTH WORLD: AN EVOLUTIONARY SELF CORRECTION

AN OVERVIEW AND CRITIQUE

Now that Ken Wilber's paper on "Trump and a Post-Truth World" is officially posted and making its rounds on the internet, I feel at liberty to share my initial "cliff notes" and comments a bit more widely.

My comments below were generated originally (and somewhat hastily) for a group of senior Wisdom students who are already working their way through this tract. It is still to be regarded as primarily a "working draft" for limited circulation, not a formal response to Ken's thesis.

The first part is a quick overview of the main points of Ken's argument as I understand it. The second part raises a few points for feedback/ critique/ further reflection.

THE ARGUMENT IN A NUTSHELL

Ken Wilber's wide-ranging and fundamentally hopeful monograph is an analysis of the recent presidential election from the perspective of *levels of consciousness* as developed primarily according to his own Integral Evolutionary Theory. The powerful contribution he brings here is to move us beyond the reactivity gripping both sides of the political spectrum and offer a much broader perspective. He proposes that Trump's upset victory reflects an "*evolutionary self-correction*" necessitated by the fact that the leading edge of consciousness, the so-called "green" level, lost its way in a mass of internal self-contradictions and gradually failed to lead. His 90-page paper is a lengthy, often verbose, occasionally brilliant analysis of how this situation came to be and what needs to happen to heal it.

To enter this discussion, one first needs to have some familiarity with the general schematic of levels of consciousness which Wilber has been steadily developing and refining for more than thirty years now (since his *Up from Eden*, first published in the early 1980s.) Wilber summarizes this in an early section of his paper, but here's the cliff notes version:

LEVELS OF CONSCIOUSNESS ARE
"COLOR CODED" AS FOLLOWS:

RED...*egocentric, self-referential, instinctual*
AMBER...*(alias "mythic membership"): ethno-*
centric, authoritarian, premodern
ORANGE...*world centric, rational, individual-*
istic, modern
GREEN...*world centric, pluralistic, postmodern*

Green, the highest evolutionary level consistently
attained to date, began to emerge in the 1960s and
has grown steadily over the next five decades, to the
point that by Wilber's estimate, some 25% of the
population are presently functioning at that level
(How does he generate this data?). But along the
way, green began to wander off course, increasingly
caught in some internal contradictions that were inherent in its worldview from the start, i.e:

1. Its inherent tendency to relativism, which pro-
gressively morphed into the claim that there is no
such thing as universal truth or universal values.
2. An inherent "performative contradiction" be-
tween its claim that all values are equal and its
inner assurance that its *value ("that there is no*
universal truth") is nonetheless normative and
binding.

31

3. A failure to distinguish between "dominator hierarchies" (based on oppression) and "growth hierarchies" (based on evolutionarily necessary differentiation), and a general dislike of all hierarchy.

4. A growingly hyper-sensitive political correctness that consistently stirred the pot of resentment and anger (both within green itself, the so-called "mean green meme," and certainly against it, among the other levels of consciousness.

This "*aperspectival madness*," as Wilber terms it, left the ostensible evolutionary leading edge caught in an increasing *cul de sac* of "nihilism and narcissism." Trump was able to successfully fan the smoldering fires of resentment building at all three lower levels––red, amber, and orange–into a roaring blaze of anti-green sentiment––an "*anti-green morphogenetic field*" that went on to torch the entire green value system. However apparently contradictory and volatile Trump's agendas may be, Wilber points out, the common denominator is that they are *always* anti-green.

Without condoning these agendas, Wilber does lay out a scenario through which it is possible to discern a coherence (I'll stop short of saying a "*justification*") behind the otherwise unfathomable upheaval that awaited the world on November 8, 2016. Rather than simply further demonizing Hillary's "basket of deplorables" that put the man in office, or re-sorting to ominous and paralyzing specters of Hitler and Armageddon, Wilber's hypothesis offers a way to make sense out of what happened—and to cooperate with evolution in making the necessary adjustments.

In the final section of his paper, Wilber does exactly that. He lays out several steps (some theoretical, others quite practical) whereby green could help heal itself and get back on track. In the end, however, Ken's conviction becomes increasingly transparent—and finally explicit—that the basic performative contradictions inherent in "green-think" are so deep as to be unsalvageable, and that *the only long term and truly satisfying solution will come only from a robust emergence of the next level of consciousness:* "Integral", *(color-coded turquoise or teal)* which is truly "second tier" (i.e., transitioning to the nondual), capable of integrating and including all perspectives, unafraid of healthy hierarchy, and hence truly able to *lead*. It is from this level, he believes, that the ultimate evolutionary resolution will emerge—once a "tipping point" of about 10% of the population functioning at that level is stabilized.

If it takes the Trump election to create this evolutionary jolt, so be it; the important thing is not to miss the window of opportunity now, that it has so dramatically opened.

COMMENTS AND CRITIQUE
FROM CYNTHIA

1. The greatest contribution of this paper is that it gets the *scale right*: it "nails" the arena in which events are actually playing out and offers a plausible hypothesis as to the underlying causes, a hypothesis which restores both coherence and an empowerment. Virtually every other analysis I have seen—political, sociological, Biblical—is working from too narrow and limited a perspective (that's the nature of intellectual discourse in the postmodern era; you either get rigor or breadth, rarely both). While I do not share all of Ken's conclusions, I am totally in agreement that the *evolutionary frame* offers our best shot at a coherent explanation and a mature and skillful resolution.

2. And as Teilhard discovered a generation before, it is at the evolutionary scale—i.e., over deep time—that *"deep hope" becomes possible*. I am gratified that Ken seems to agree with Teilhard that evolution is intrinsically purposeful (and in much the same terms as Teilhard sees it: moving toward greater "complexification/consciousness"–

–not specifically so-named—and an ever-fuller manifestation of Love (or "Eros," in Wilber languaging). I wish Teilhard were more generally cited in Wilber's work; it would certainly draw the dual streams of Teilhardian and Integral evolutionary theory into a more creative and ultimately illumining dialogue.

3. I continue to suspect that Wilber often conflates "levels of consciousness" with "stages of growth." The two are not identical, at least according to the criteria I have gleaned from my own Christian contemplative heritage. I remain to be convinced that orange and green are actually different levels; to me they look more like simply *progressive stages of the same level.* Orange may be individualistic while green is pluralistic, but both are relying on the mental egoic operating system ("perception through differentiation") to run their program; green's "groups" therefore, are merely "individuals writ large," (which "*co-exist*") not a new holonic unity (which "*coalesces.*") Or another way of saying it: green is simply orange looking through a postmodern filter.

This, incidentally, I believe to be another

fatal "performative contradiction" unde-
tected by Wilber; greens think *for* oneness
but *from* "perception through differentiation." How crazy-making is that? It's a
pretty significant developmental gap to
navigate, causing their minds always to be
out ahead of what their psyches can actually maintain. Hence the anger, the arrogance, and the hypocrisy.

4. I'm no political historian, but I think
Wilber takes some pretty large leapfrogs
through the history of the political parties
in the US. I'd be highly skeptical that he
can make his assertion stick that Demo-
crats by and large function in a higher level
of consciousness (green/orange) than Re-
publicans (orange/amber). This may be
true of the past few decades, but given that
prior to its infiltration by the Religious
Right, The Republican party was more often the standard bearer for the leading
edge of consciousness (case in point:
Abraham Lincoln), while the Democratic
party was the home to most ethnicities and
nearly all of the South. Thus, it's difficult
to see how it would be without its share of
well-entrenched ethnocentric (amber) perspectives.

5. Finally, and most substantively, the most important corrective the Christian mystical tradition has to bring to current secular or Buddhist-based models of "second tier" (and higher) states of consciousness is the *insistence that the leap to this new level of conscious functioning is not simply an extension of the cognitive line but requires "putting the mind in the heart," not only attitudinally but neurologically.* There is a supporting physiology to each tier of consciousness (which is why I think green and orange are still basically at the same level), and that all-important shift from 1st tier to 2nd tier will only happen when grounded in an active awakening of the heart.

And this means, basically, it will happen in the domain of *devotion*—i.e., our heart's emotional assent and participation in the ultimate "thouness" of the cosmos and the experiential certainty of the divine not simply as "love" but as *Lover*. That is to say, I believe it happens beyond the gates of secularity, in the intense, holographic particularity of the upper echelons in each sacred tradition. This is for me the profound strength of Teilhard's model, as over and against Wilber's more secular model; it unabashedly is able to stir the fires of adoration and spiritual imagination as it "harnesses the energy of love." Striving to light this same fire with metaphysical matches, Wilber is left essentially "anthropomorphizing" evolution, transforming it into a new version of the classic *demiurge*, the creative and implementing arm of the logoic omniscience.

I look forward to hearing your comments and feedback. I repeat: this is a groundbreaking and heartening essay, at the right scale, and headed in the right direction. It's worth taking the time to grapple with.

~January 30, 2017
Northeast Wisdom at northeastwisdom.org

THE BELLRACK

Over these past two decades of spiritual teaching, I have found myself increasingly bumping up against the hard edges of two core assumptions that frame the way we typically understand transformation.

The first is the assumption that spirituality is an *ascent*. The way to God is "up," and the most keenly sought after spiritual states are "higher." The dominant metaphor is the ladder, and as with all ladders, the goal is to get to the top.

The second is the well-nigh universal habit of setting up the spiritual journey in terms of an *interior combat*, with the mortal enemy typically identified as the "ego" or "false self," a distorted but tenacious part of our own being. This assumption drives the pervasive use of the metaphor of *spiritual warfare*, where the goal of transformation is to vanquish, silence, "dismantle," or in some other way override that lower self which—in the words of *The Course in Miracles*—"wants you dead."

Now there is deep wisdom to be gleaned from the Mad Hatter's celebrated assertion, "How you get there is where you'll arrive." Those two master metaphors of axial spirituality set us down in a spiritual terrain marked by oppositionality, judgment, competitiveness, and implicitly (sometimes *explicitly*), violence. Now if spiritual transformation is fundamentally about growth, basic common sense will tell you that this is not the optimal environment in which for things to grow. The path of "internal warfare" has certainly produced its spiritual heroes, but has also reaped more than its share of vainglory, repression, self-righteousness, and fear.

Is there a kinder and gentler way of framing transformation?

As I pondered this question, I discovered that my alternative metaphor was literally ringing in my ears. Many years ago, when I spent a season of my life as an ecumenical fellow at St John's Abbey, that great Benedictine mother ship nestled lakeside in rural Minnesota, my ears soon became attuned to the clamor of the great bell rack erupting periodically throughout the day. Over the entrance to the imposing, Marcel Breuer designed Abbey Church stood an enormous concrete bell banner housing four bells of different sizes and timbres (none of them less than five hundred pounds, I'd guess; we are talking *huge* here!) Several times a day, but with particular gusto right before daily mass at 5 pm, the grand hullabaloo would begin. One bell would get rolling, then the three others would join in their turn, until finally the whole countryside was wrapped in a massive sonorous tapestry. Throughout the entire year at St. John's I never grew tired of those bells, which always seemed to be calling me back, not only to the deeper rhythms of Benedictine *ora et labora*, but to something deeper within myself.

Well there it was, I realized, my alternative metaphor for selfhood: *the bell rack!* Not a higher self and a lower self locked in mortal combat, not a merciless race to the spiritual top, but a family of different sizes, shapes, and timbres all contributing their unique melody to the whole.

I will introduce each of these four bells shortly and explain a bit more about how this alternative metaphor works, but first let me fill in one more key piece of the backstory. A major turning point in my own journey of transformation came about twenty years ago, in the course of some very intense shadow work undertaken with my beloved jousting partner, Brother Raphael Robin. Prior to that time, as a good student of Centering Prayer, I had been patiently working to dismantle my false self, assuming that my "true self" would be what was left when the illusory pretender was exposed. But as the raw intimacy of the work with Rafe intensified, we both began to notice that it was not the best side of ourselves that God seemed to be calling forth in the crucible of transformation, but strangely, the *worst*—maybe because that's where the seeds of our redeemed essence were in fact planted. My desperate clinging and grasping that so dogged the path of our relationship would eventually reemerge in the transforming fires as an authentic capacity for devotion. His towering isolation turned out to guard the threshold to an almost unbearably tender compassion. Throw out the bathwater, and out goes the baby with it!

Through the work with Rafe I gradually came to see that that much maligned "false self" is really our *protector*-self—and in a strange way, the reverse mirror of our capacity for transformation. It's extraordinary what lengths a vulnerable and wounded human being will go to, what intricate psychic armor he or she will construct in order to remain in the game of life, not to be overcome by despair. In that sense, this *nafs* (as the Sufis call this "lower passional self") really carries the force of our *hope*, our stubborn courage to hang in even when the odds seem hopelessly stacked against us. The goal, then, is not to dismantle it but to *transfigure* it, reclaiming the essence qualities it has so valiantly defended. That was a huge turning point in my own spiritual journey, a whole new way of looking at myself and others.

And so in my bellrack, I do indeed call this first bell my *nafs*, my "lower passional self." I prefer this to the term "false self," for there is absolutely nothing false about this self (except in comparison to some hypothetical "true self"). It is empirically real. It is an ancient and valid part of my being. And it is not my enemy. Nafs is my functional storefront for dealing with the issues of the world, meeting life head on, and keeping things moving along the horizontal axis. And typically, until one has extensive spiritual work under one's belt, it is the principal source of my *personal agency*; nothing much is going to get done in life without its cooperation.

The second bell in my bellrack I call *Soul*. Soul is the voice of the artist and lover in me, the cosmic gambler, the Delphic oracle who believes that beneath the shifting sands of daily life there is a deeper pattern at work, a truer version of who I am, waiting patiently to be discovered. Soul speaks to me in a thousand voices: in dreams and archetypes, in shades of value, in the richness of the emotive life, in the siren call to authenticity. There is always an aspect of hiddenness here; she must be discovered and teased out from among the thousand mirages of nafs-ordered life. But when you get her right, it is always with that rich sense of "coming round to where we began and knowing the place for the first time."

Soul is the true feeling of myself *from the perspective of my finite selfhood*—or in other words, as viewed through the lens of my self-reflective consciousness. It is the deepest and truest story of me. But it is, in the end, a *story*: the reflected light of something far more allusive and real, to which it points through the hall of mirrors of my *faculties*, that is to say, my memory, reason, imagination, feeling, and will.

The third bell in my bellrack I call *Spirit*. But in fact, this is not really "my" bell at all; it does not belong to "me." Spirit is seamless and indivisible; it really belongs only to God. As it enters our being (at conception), it turns on the lights of our individual animation and dwells within us as the animating principle and the specific reminder of that which is infinite within us. Sometimes it floods us with drenching downloads of unboundaried consciousness. "I am *that*," I exclaim. But truly, I will never "become" spirit. It dwells in us, and through that indwelling, connects us to the formless, to that "high lonesome" waiting to be gentled and personalized in form ("*apprivoiser*," says Le Petit Prince). To paraphrase that old cliché, it is the Divine having a human experience.

Heart is my last bell. And here things get a bit more complicated, for heart shares many traits with soul, yet has a distinctly different flavor. If soul is the sense of myself generated through my finite operating system—i.e., through *reflecting* on my being—

44

heart is what happens when I simply and purely *coincide* with my being, when the ocean enters the drop. The view is holographic rather than linear; there are still specific essence qualities to my being, but they do not *define* me, let alone differentiate me from others. Comparison/contrast has dropped out; the journal remains unopened.

Heart is concrete, particular, practical, often surprising. Unlike soul, it is not insistent or fussy. Its wellbeing does not depend on a specific set of external conditions; rather, it comes roaring in from the infinite filling every nook and cranny of any and all conditions with the fullness of its being. It is the lion in winter in the cave of my heart, and when it wakes up and begins to roar, the whole bellrack explodes in a single harmonic offering.

It is also the true seat of the *personal*—or in other words, of the dynamic, relational aliveness that emerges when one's being is entirely "sounded through" ("*per-sonare*") by one's *true* true self, which does not belong to this earth plane. As Black Elk would say, it is "the shadow cast on earth by yonder vision in the heaven, so bright it is, so clear." Heart is the angel of my Being.

I've written elsewhere about my "Four Voices" method of spiritual discernment, based on listening appreciatively to each voice in the inner bellrack. If you'd like, you can take my online course on it on

45

the Contemplative Journal website. Some people tell me that they have found this approach helpful. For now, however, I want to stick with this present assignment, which is to talk about transformation.

You remember how I spoke earlier about those two underlying assumptions that jointly frame our understanding of transformation. To these I would now like to add a third, closely related to the other two: the assumption that *the purpose of our sojourn here on earth is to earn admission to somewhere else, somewhere better.* Call it heaven, nirvana, the nondual realm, the name does not matter; the bottom line is the same. Again and again that neoplatonic siren call of "spiritualization" (the ladder ready at hand) seduces us onward and upward again, away from the simple, incarnational epicenter of our Christian faith: "for God so *loved* the world that he gave his only son."

But if we really come back to center and view our world through Christ-rooted eyes, we come to see that this earth-plane is not a waiting room for heaven (or a final exam to see if we qualify); it is the place where certain aspects of love which can only be spoken in form and finitude are indeed spoken, resonating simultaneously through all realms, visible and invisible. I am thinking here about qualities such as fidelity, steadfastness, and most particularly about what I call *Eucharistic love*: the capacity to have your heart broken wide open without resorting to despair or bitterness. These are subtle essences of love that

46

can only be woven on the warp of time and the weft of finitude. But they are the most tender and hidden facets of the heart of our Common Father—"the treasure longing to be known," as the Sufi's call it—and it is our tremendous privilege and honor here on this earth plane to be able to play that love song on the lute strings of our own heart.

Strange isn't it, how we spend so much of our spiritual energy trying to get out of human form when all along it seems that God's real wish is for us to get *into* it.

Whatever you make of this paradox, it's hard to deny that our human psyche does seems to be perfectly anatomically wired for the job of bridging the realms: mediating between the infinite and the finite; the universal and the particular; the gross world of form and the more subtle realms, in a marvelous and mysterious two-way street. Almost as if it were deliberately set up that way. And in this mysterious cosmic assignment, if that's what it is, the finite parts of our selfhood are as vital and indispensable as our high-soaring infinite yearnings, and the tension between these two perspectives must not be collapsed, but rather, consciously borne. As that late great wisewoman Helen Luke once famously remarked, "Wholeness is born out of the acceptance of the conflict of human and divine in the individual psyche."

Not suppression of the conflict, but *acceptance* of it, as part of the sacred task of being a human being. If that's your map of transformation, as it has become mine, then the goal is to welcome *all* the voices, all perspectives, all the blessed ways in which we spontaneously hold dual citizenship in both the finite and the formless realms. And rooted and grounded in both, we do our best to live here worthily and with gusto, to bless and upload the fruits of our finitude directly into the divine heart—which is not "up," incidentally, but rather "*all*:" the entire cosmic bell rack.

And so, speaking of bellracks, I can only end by yielding the floor to Leonard Cohen, whose vision almost perfectly encapsulates what I understand by transformation:

Ring out the bells that still can ring
Forget your perfect offering
There is a crack in everything
That's how the light gets in.

~Spring 2017
Oneing Volume 5, No 1
Center for Action and Contemplation

THE HEART OF COMPASSION: EXPLORING THE INTERIOR LANDSCAPE

What I want to do here today, is actually raise a couple of questions and perspectives on the heart of compassion. It is more of a question than it is a statement.

I think one of the real problems that we get into when we try, particularly in the west, to understand compassion, is that a lot of people have a hard time distinguishing it from pity or from charity—or from being a helper. What happens is that, as we tend to understand compassion, it implies a subtle power differential. Very often we place ourselves— through identification—on the side of the "haves." We are the ones who are practicing compassion, we are the doers and then there are the "done untos." It is like that great prayer: "*Thank God, I am not like other men, but there for the grace of God go I.*" Well, drop out the "but for the grace of God" and "there go I" and you are closer to the truth.

How do we eliminate the power differential? True compassion is not like that at all. True compassion is like love—like eros—in that it levels the playing field. True compassion creates out of what were hierarchical human relationships, a single wholeness.

The final result of compassion—of a compassionate action—is that there is the healing and the empowerment of the whole. Of course, Jesus was right on to this. One of the most popular of his teachings, is the powerful parable of the good Samaritan, where "the haves" walked right by the person in distress and it was the one who was "the have not," the Samaritan, the pariah, who was actually able to break the trap. I think what Jesus was saying there was, "Watch out, watch out. Don't place yourself in the position of the entitled one, of the helping one, of the powerful one, the strong one. Turn the table upside down and see what you get."

We all know "love your neighbor as yourself," but we always hear that as "love your neighbor as much as yourself." And then you have, "But, I have to love myself, first." We don't realize is that there is no comparison there. Love your neighbor as yourself—one individual. It is fundamentally an act of seeing. The doing will fall out of the seeing. We don't see from the oneness—we don't know *how* to see from the oneness—we don't even know that we're not seeing from the oneness. And aye, there's the dilemma, the rub. *What do you do about that?*

In the spiritual traditions that I come from, which is basically the Christian tradition, informed deeply by the Sufi tradition, we have a teaching about something called *identification*. It is a form of an attachment, attachment to your sense of self, to your self-image, or, even deeper, your sense of persona. It is your image of yourself—as a helper, or as a compassionate person, or as a victim.

We carry these little identifications inside and we don't see them, and we don't want to see them. Particularly in the Western tradition that most of us have grown up steeped in—we actually use *attachment*—as the motivator for righteous action. We can't imagine righteous action happening apart from attachment. It's the Old Testament model, zeal for the Lord is burning up the house.

We identify ourselves with the good person, with the moral high ground, with the right, with the one who is God's little helper. With the one that is doing the right thing. I don't think anybody ever self-identifies as the one who is doing the wrong thing. We subtly steal the moral high ground. And we don't even see we are doing it.

As a matter of fact, people say, "Look at Jesus throwing the money changers out of the temple. You have to be angry, you have to have a sense of justice in order to be able to act righteously and compassionately in the world." This tradition says, "*No*, not so." That is actually the blinder that's always introducing the power differential and skewing compassion into pity and do-gooding.

One of the most powerful quotes I know comes from a Christian teacher, now dead, Gerald May, who was involved with the Shalem Institute for Spiritual Formation. He has a wonderfully challenging koan in his book Will and Spirit. He says:

> *As attachment ceases to be your motivation, your actions will become reflections of compassion absolute.*

"As attachment ceases to be your motivation, your actions will become reflections of compassion absolute." It's amazing, what he's saying. In other words, your attachment is the blind spot—the thumb over the camera lens. As you let go of attachment, what you begin to see is that the world actually is Rahim—it is the womb—the fundamental nature of reality. Whether you call it God, Interdependent Arising, whatever you name it, it is ordered and structured; it is relational, it is personal—it is *compassionate*.

Once you see that, that tidal wave of the actual fundamental nature of reality is what rises up to carry you into a compassionate action. An action which is judgement-free and without role playing. To see the world as one, to see the world as coherent and compassionate, is the challenge, is that amazing flick of the light bulb.

What our western tradition has said very clearly here, is that *only the heart* can see that fundamental nature of reality. The mind can never see the world as a coherent, unconditioned whole. That requires the heart to kick in, the heart as it is understood in the west, not as source of emotion, not even as a source of empathy, but as an organ of spiritual perception which perceives by vibrational resonance. By being able to enter the insides of things, and sense *holographically* the pattern from the whole. Over and over in the west comes the refrain: "*Put the mind in the heart; put the mind in the heart.*" Which doesn't mean get out of your mental constructions and start "feeling." What it means in scientific language, which my friends in the neurology business say we can begin to measure—is to entrain the rhythms and the vibrational field of the brain to the vibrational field of the heart—so they form a single instrument of perception.

Over and over spiritual practice says, "*Put the mind in the heart, put the mind in the heart.*" As that happens, the conditioned self, that busy translator, acting, doing good, participating, motivating is—gone. What you begin to see on the inside is that the world looks intimate. *Intimacy* is the feeling tone, is the objective real description of the world seen from the perspective of the heart. There is an intimate belongingness—a cohesiveness—a coherence from the field. When you look at the world from the heart, and see the intimacy, action flows out as effortless compassion. *Effortless compassion* is the external side of the coin, of which the internal is *heart-perceived intimacy.*

Another phrase for that kind of a condition might be "to work out of *conscience.*" I would like to introduce this word and ask us to reclaim it, to taste it. We confuse conscience with morality, or with blurred social norms, or with that little voice that beats upon you all day, saying you should do this, you must do that. *Conscience is simply the heart center.* The eye of the heart wide open, perceiving the scale of things. Perceiving the love. The equalizing, leveling, love that flows through everything. Pulling it into one.

When we see from that eye of conscience, we see from the oneness, we see from the humility, we see from the compassion that flows out into world in a whole new way. The point of the spiritual practice to *put the mind in the heart* is to try to open up the conditions and help us remember the practices that move us from that mental, calculating, acting, identified self into simply being. In that oneness that can see, and what I truly believe, that compassion does not belong to the individual even. *It is an emergent property of the whole.* And as we realign and reorient

54

and reground ourselves in the whole—*compassion flows*.

The last image I will leave you with is this. We are here in Louisville. It's my first time in Louisville, but I have known Louisville for years from Thomas Merton. My hotel is right on the corner of what used to be 4th and Walnut, in the middle of the shopping district, where Merton realized: "*I loved all these people.*" I could not be separate from them. "*They were mine, and I theirs.*" Merton said:

> *I woke from this funny and spurious dream of belonging to this small, special realm and I could say "Thank God! Thank God, I am like other men."*

It is from that seeing, that everything shifted in Merton's life. It was the watershed epiphany in his life, and all of a sudden, he moved from pity, charity, and compassion as something you did, to the natural flowing of this different kind of seeing.

His final words in that beautiful statement:

> *I have no formula for that seeing, but the gates of heaven are everywhere.*

So, in this city, in this place, on this occasion, I would merely ask us to believe, that when, as the tradition says, our sense of self comes down into the heart, something opens that allows the rest to flow from a new place. As we are able to do that, we shift the art and science of compassion to a whole new ground. Keep striving and working for that transpersonal, personal, openness of the heart. And the rest—the gates of heaven—are everywhere. Thank you.

~April 21 2017
Festival of Faiths, Louisville, Kentucky

TEILHARD FOR TROUBLED TIMES

PART I: DEEP HOPE FLOWS OVER DEEP TIME

I don't know what kind of divine nudge it may have been that prompted me in January 2015 to challenge the students in my Wisdom network to a deep dive into Teilhard, but the response was electric, to say the least. Over the ensuing eighteen months we collectively chomped our way through *The Human Phenomenon*, *The Divine Milieu*, and *The Heart of Matter* in both online formats and on-the-ground Wisdom schools and retreats. Students who really caught the Teilhard bug read even more widely, exploring the entire range of his canon from the magnificent early mystical upwellings in *Writings in Time of War* to the profound final synthesis in *The Christic*, completed less than a month before his death.

So the cornerstones were all in place by November 2016—and not a moment too soon, I might add.

Without straying too far into politics, I can simply report that within the circles I mostly travel in, the response to the upset election victory of Donald Trump has been one of shock, disorientation, and a gathering sense of doom. Not only does it appear that the progressive social and environmental values that have set the political agenda for nearly six decades are being systematically deconstructed; the even more fundamental *moral* values—truthfulness, compassion, integrity, conscience—now seem themselves to be under attack. In a brave new world of "alternative facts," "fake news," and a rising tide of belligerence and vulgarity it seems as if human consciousness is going backwards. How could this have happened, and how do we come to terms with a future that suddenly feels much darker and more precarious?

It is just here that Teilhard enters the equation, offering a vastly broader and more hopeful perspective in which to search for a new moral resolve. Writing in a historical era whose traumatic upheavals eerily foreshadow our own (and in whose unresolved anguish lie the roots of so much of our postmodern skepticism and despair), he is yet able to paint a bigger picture where there is still room for optimism and coherence. As I've drawn out these Teilhardian "way-points" before a variety of audiences, I have found that people are deeply comforted and encouraged by his perspective. Amidst the welter of analysis (sociological, historical, psychological, political) being thrown at our present situation by the secular intelligentsia, there is simply not enough breadth and depth of vision to reveal the deeper processes from which hope emerges. That is precisely the missing piece Teilhard is so powerfully able to bring. In this three-part series, *Teilhard for Troubled Times*, I would like to call attention to three points in particular, all foundational pieces of the so-called "Teilhardian Synthesis," that have already proved to be powerful starting points for reorientation and renewed hope as our planet begins to re-group.

First of all, Teilhard reminds us that "*deep hope flows over deep time.*" From his perspective as a geologist and paleontologist, he reassures us that evolution has not changed direction; it has always been and always will be "a rise toward consciousness" (HP 183), moving irreversibly toward its consummation at the Omega point. But its span is measured in eons, not decades. When we try to "cinch up on the bat" too tightly or lose sight of the cosmic scale, the result is anguish. If we measure human progress only by our usual historical benchmarks—the last eight years of Obama initiatives, the eighty years of FDR social safety nets, the not-yet 250 years of the American democratic experiment—or for that matter, the "mere" 2500 years of Western civilization; we are still only catching the inevitable play of what Teilhard calls tatonnement, or "trial and error;" part of the necessary play of freedom. Even the emergence of human consciousness itself, he reminds us, reaching its present configuration a mere 125,000 years ago with the stunning debut of *homo sapiens*, was preceded by a 10,000-year ice age, in which it appeared that all that had been gained prior to that point was irreversibly lost. It wasn't. No sooner had the ice receded than the first irrefutable paleontological manifestations confirm that human beings were now using fire and tools—unmistakable evidence that beneath the ice and apparent desolation, the evolutionary journey was still unperturbedly marching forward.

Perhaps that feels like a false hope. Perhaps it is bought at the cost of all sensitivity to individual suffering and pain, by setting the scale at so vast a magnitude that human lives register as no more than as tiny pixels. Teilhard was accused of exactly that in his writings after World War II, when Europe, still reeling from the horror of the holocaust and Hiroshima, was overwhelmed by personal and collective remorse. He was accused of false optimism, of an indifference to personal suffering. But Teilhard was by no means indifferent. His life-transforming vision of the oneness of humanity came in the midst of serving as stretcher bearer in the bloody trenches of World War I, and his writings on human progress rose from the untold depths of personal suffering he endured in faithfulness to a vocation and a Church that actively blocked his path. He knew personal suffering only too well, and he looked straight into the face of the sorrow, the horror, and named it as such. The haunting prayer woven into his reflection on faith in *The Divine Milieu* (112) makes clear that it is no cheap optimism he is dispensing here, but a wrenchingly honest acknowledgement of our human predicament:

> *Ah, you know it yourself, Lord, through having borne the anguish of it as a man: on certain days the world seems a terrifying thing: huge, blind, and brutal. It buffets us about, drags us along, and kills us with complete indifference. Heroically, it may truly be said, man has contrived to create a more or less habitable zone of light and warmth in the midst of the cold, dark waters—a zone where people have eyes to see, hands to help, and hearts to love. But how precarious that habitation is! At any moment, the vast and horrible thing may break in through the cracks—the thing we try hard to forget is always there, separated from us by a flimsy partition: fire, pestilence, storms, earth-quakes. Or the unleashing of dark moral forces— these callously sweep away in one moment what we have laboriously built up and beautified with all our intelligence and all our love.*

But he knew that to capitulate to anguish was to lose the thread, and this he would not permit. The deeper ley lines of resilience and hope were alive and well for him, safely sealed within the deep, telluric memory of the earth itself and the Christic impulse beaconing from the future. But the road rises on the other side of despair. Allowing oneself to be engulfed in either anger or grief amounts to a fatal loss of moral nerve and hence a betrayal of the evolutionary task entrusted to our species.

I want to conclude by making clear that I do not see this "deep hope" as an excuse to relax our vigilance in stewardship for the planet earth. Teilhard does not permit himself to be used that way; his sense of the oneness of the earth and of its dynamic interwovenness pervades everything he sees and writes. But he realizes as well that Mother Earth has an intelligence and a resilience that meets us far more than halfway, and that frantic efforts to "save the earth" are likely to be more about saving our own skins. Over the millennia our planet has endured meteor strikes, the rise and fall of sea levels, ice ages, the continual shifting of tectonic plates, the appearance and disappearance of species. We *homo sapiens* may indeed become one of those "lost species" if in our greed and arrogance we bring about planetary conditions that no longer support the uncomfortably tight tolerances in which human life is actually sustainable. But even if that unthinkable should occur, evolution itself will not be derailed. The earth itself, infinitely adaptable, will continue on, and the species that inevitably arises to replace us will bear in its cosmic memory the trousseau of all that consciousness has attained in this evolutionary go-round.

For sure, we need to fall on our knees every morning and beseech our mother Earth to help carry us through this latest dark time of human greed and destructiveness. But our real task at this evolutionary cusp is *not to lose sight of what is coming to us from the future*, the vision of our common humanity that is indeed "groaning and travailing" to be born. That will be the subject of Part II of this series.

~April 3, 2017
The Omega Center at omegacenter.info

TEILHARD FOR TROUBLED TIMES

PART II: DON'T CO-EXIST, COALESCE!

The second hopeful resource that Teilhard brings to our unsettled political times is his unshakable conviction that evolutionary progress will unfold its ultimate triumph in the realm of the *personal*. While our postmodern temperament has a well ingrained tendency to regard the world through a filter of distrust, in which the bits and pieces inevitably appear "random" and disconnected—certainly *impersonal*—Teilhard encourages us to see our planetary home as a coherent and increasingly compassionate whole, steadily plying its way along its irreversible evolutionary trajectory. In the big picture, there is nothing to suggest that evolution has gone off track. But there is plenty to suggest that we are entering a critical new phase in which some old-order planetary survival strategies are giving way to a new and more intentional sense of mutual interdependence.

Early on in Teilhard's *The Human Phenomenon*, in the course of a powerful philosophical reflection on "The Ways of Life," (HP 65-68), he acknowledges that one of the characteristics of life as it voraciously emerges on our young planet is its "indifference toward individuals." The evolutionary trajectory over its inaugural billions of years has been far more skewed toward collective survival than individual wellbeing—"Life is more real than lives," as Teilhard un-flinchingly observes (HP, p. 67). But that pattern may now be starting to shift as human beings, more and more consciously awakening to the sway of Omega (the ultimate convergence of all things in love), willingly embark on the next leg of the evolutionary journey that will transform them from individuals into *persons*.

How's that again? We typically use these terms interchangeably, but for Teilhard they denote distinctly different, progressive evolutionary stages.

An *individual* lives as an autonomous unit, subject to the old-order laws of "survival of the fittest" and planetary indifference. A *person* has come to understand himself or herself as belonging to a greater relational field in which individual autonomy defers to a flowing give-and-take that allows the whole unit to function at a much higher order of coherence: a whole greater than the sum of its parts. In this greater whole both unity and differentiation are preserved; meanwhile, the symbiotic union between the whole and the part drives the evolutionary dynamo toward even more powerful expressions of consciousness and love—or in other words, ever more firmly into the realm of the personal. When we are fully there, Teilhard boldly predicts in *The Human Phenomenon*, yet another cosmic threshold will have been crossed as:

> ...*the world's indifference to its elements will be transformed into an immense solicitude—in the sphere of the person.(67)*

"But we are not there yet," he cautions. The journey toward this next evolutionary benchmark is still barely underway, and at the stage we're at, three steps forward are still regularly matched by two steps back. Yet for all the bumps in the road, the vision of that higher collectivity he first glimpsed in the trenches of World War I guided Teilhard like a pole star throughout his life, both galvanizing his imagination and enflaming his heart. It can do the same for us, even in our own sad and distrustful times.

A cautionary note, however: for Teilhard, oneness does not equate simply to some sentimental proclamation of fellowship or "let's all just get along." It is firmly grounded in his master evolutionary principle, the Law of Complexification/Consciousness. According to the law, every new benchmark of consciousness as it manifests here on earth is accompanied by—or in other words, *correlative with*—the emergence of a higher, more articulated physical form (Teilhard calls it an "arrangement") that serves as its vehicle. This implies, if I catch his drift correctly—and in distinct contrast to the model commonly promulgated in most schools of spiritual enlightenment today—that the breakthrough to what is now popularly called "nondual consciousness" will not come as the result of a series of *individual* enlightenments, but in the emergence of a new organic body of humanity, a *mystical* body of humanity. This new organic whole will display the signature "differentiation-within-unity" that Teilhard variously refers to as "cephalization" or *centration*. It will have a "head," i.e., a distinctly recognizable command post or seat of consciousness, around which its diverse components will self-organize—in a fashion not unlike like St. Paul's stunningly prescient vision in 1 Corinthians (12: 14-26) of the "many members of the one body of Christ":

> *Indeed, the body does not consist of one member but of many. If the foot were to say, "Because I am not a hand, I do not belong to the body," that would not make it any less a part of the body. And if the ear were to say, "Because I am not an eye, I do not belong to the body," that would not*

67

make it any less a part of the body. If the whole body were an eye, where would the hearing be? If the whole body were hearing, where would the sense of smell be? As it is, there are many members, yet one body. The eye cannot say to the hand, "I have no need of you," nor again the head to the feet, "I have no need of you"... if one member suffers, all suffer together with it; if one member is honored, all rejoice together with it.

This new organic body of humanity, its corporeity primarily carried in the *noosphere*, will guide and shape—is *already* guiding and shaping—the emerging consciousness of humanity. It is serenely undisturbed by the rise and fall of political tyrants and the final paroxysms of religious and nationalistic tribalism. The rising scent of our common humanity is already in the air, and as we consciously join hearts across the antiquated boundaries of the nationalities and denominations that once defined our identities, the blue biosphere of our planet earth is being superseded and suffused with the gold and scarlet of our common human heart coursing toward its Omega.

I offer this Teilhardian vision as a source of renewed hope in a world that seems, at the moment, to be moving aggressively toward an intensified retrenchment and fragmentation. The downturn cannot last, Teilhard would have us see; the evolutionary current has already swept us beyond it. And indeed, we can already see moving beneath the troubled waters the unmistakable harbingers of this dawning human oneness. We see it in the worldwide demonstrations that spontaneously broke out on January 21, 2017 in solidarity with the Women's March in DC. We see it in the outpouring of concern for refugees and dispossessed in Syria and elsewhere, in the snowballing movement of churches and city governments to declare themselves sanctuary zones, and in the skillful, understated way that the other governments of the world have so far largely been able to work together to contain the Trump administration like a giant oil slick. The gathering body of universal compassion is not about to let itself be dismantled! And there is indeed reason for hope that the rising star of human oneness, announced by Teilhard nearly a hundred years ago, has by now reached sufficient stability in its noetic orbit to carry us through this present rough patch and onward toward Omega. At any rate, that is where we need to place our hope and our best efforts: in the continued, patient cultivation of our common humanity.

We will see in Part III of this series why this is already an empirical reality.

~April 17, 2017
The Omega Center at omegacenter.info

TEILHARD FOR TROUBLED TIMES

PART III: THE LIVING REALITY
OF OMEGA

The third and most powerful wellspring of hope that Teilhard has to offer us—for those with "eyes to see and hearts to hear"—is the assurance that this slow toiling of the planet toward Omega is not merely some hypothetical, futuristic theory. Omega is neither abstract nor hypothetical; it is already present, actively suffusing and permeating the earth with its telluric energy. "I probably would never have dared to consider or form the rational hypothesis of it," Teilhard writes in *The Human Phenomenon*, "if I had not already found in my consciousness as a believer not only the speculative model for it, but its living reality." (HP 211).

That "living reality," is of course, the radiant heart of Christ, which Teilhard first met as a child and which continued to grow in him throughout his life as a palpably real and personal presence. Not only his own heart, but the entire planet, were increasingly enfolded within the immediately experiential realm of "the Christic."

There are those, I realize, for whom this aspect of Teilhard is uncomfortable. Many contemporary Teilhardian scholars—indeed, some of the most prominent among them—see as their goal the necessary "secularization" of Teilhard, extrapolating from his grand mystical synthesis the elements that will stand on their own as hard evolutionary science. Teilhard himself does not discourage this demarcation (he set up *The Human Phenomenon* so that his explicit comments about "The Christian Phenomena" are confined to the epilogue), and in light of the rigid and frozen dogmatism that is so often mistaken for "faith" in the popular estimation, demarcation is perhaps a necessary starting point. But I am personally convinced that in the long term it does no service to the ultimate impact of Teilhard's vision; the vision's coherence is weakened and its real sources of validation are obscured. In the grand tapestry of Teilhardian seeing, the warp of science and the weft of mysticism are inextricably intertwined. And it is just here, in fact, that Teilhard's greatest gift to our own troubled times may lie waiting to be tapped.

To the very end of his life, Teilhard kept on his writing desk an icon of the radiant heart of Christ. I have a copy of that icon on my own writing desk right now, and I am constantly surprised by how its quiet presence continues to call me up short. From the center of Christ's chest the energy pulsates out in radiant waves, serenely carrying the world toward its consummation in Omega.

It was Teilhard's *felt-sense* conviction of the presence of Christ already at work in "the stuff of the universe," directing the course of evolution from within its very planetary marrow, that allowed him over a lifetime of otherwise unbearable diminishments to "stay the course," bearing untold personal suffering for the sake of a world that was already luminously inhabited by Christ; in fact, his very body. In Part I, I quoted from Teilhard's searing meditation on the indifference and uncertainty of this world:

> *Ah, you know it yourself, Lord, through having borne the anguish of it as a man: on certain days the world seems a terrifying thing: huge, blind, and brutal. It buffets us about, drags us along, and kills us with complete indifference. Heroically, it may truly be said, man has contrived to create a more or less habitable zone of light and warmth in the midst of the cold, dark waters—a zone where people have eyes to see, hands to help, and hearts to love. But how precarious that habitation is! At any moment, the vast and horrible thing may break in through the cracks—the thing we try*

hard to forget is always there, separated from us by a flimsy partition: fire, pestilence, storms, earthquakes. Or the unleashing of dark moral forces—these callously sweep away in one moment what we have laboriously built up and beautified with all our intelligence and all our love.

That is merely the first paragraph, however. In the second he offers his response—quintessentially Teilhardian—as he takes refuge in that intimate, pan-eucharistic presence of Christ, sensed through the eyes of faith:

Since my dignity as a man, O God, forbids me to close my eyes to this—like an animal or a child—that I may not succumb to the temptation to curse the universe and him who made it, teach me to adore it by seeing you concealed within it. O Lord, repeat to me the great liberating words, the words which at once reveal and operate: Hoc est corpus meum (this is my body). In truth, the huge and dark thing, the phantom, the storm—if we want it to be so, is you! Ego sum; nolite timere ("It is I; do not be afraid.") The things in our life that terrify us, the things which threw you yourself into agony in the garden, are, ultimately, only the species or appearance, the matter of one and the same sacrament.

73

For Teilhard, faith is not a matter of assent to a rationally derived set of doctrines and principles. It is first and foremost an *action*–an "operative" as he calls it—which is set in motion when one steps up to the plate and looks squarely in the face of reversal and evil through the radiance of that experienced Christic reality. My own spiritual teacher, the monastic hermit Brother Rafe, called this stance a "wager:" if the premise is true, you will live it into action. Rather than trying to do faith from the "top down," by first convincing yourself of the logical plausibility of the argument in question, begin from the "bottom up," *by acting in alignment with it*, and see what happens next!

There is a certain "Heisenberg" quality at work in all this, Teilhard insinuates in his brilliant reflection on faith in *The Divine Milieu* (though of course, without invoking Heisenberg's celebrated uncertainty principle directly). The quality of our presence does indeed impact the overall energetic field, with the results measured not so much in the sphere of outcome as in the overall "quickening" (he calls it "suranimation") of the relational field itself. Events are not necessarily transformed, but *meaning* is transformed. When subjected to the softening and harmonizing energy of faith, the hard edges of physical reality soften, become more supple, come into responsivity and coherence:

Chance is seen to be order, success assumes incor-
ruptible plenitude, suffering becomes a caress of
God. (DM, 111)

"But if we hesitate," he continues, "the rock remains dry, the sky dark, the waters treacherous and
shifting"—or in other words, the universe continues
to appear indifferent, disconnected, and unresponsive—"and we may hear the voice of the Master,
faced with our bungled lives: 'O men of little faith,
why have you doubted...?' "

It is the universal Christic presence—already
seeded into the universe through the incarnation,
catalyzed in the Paschal Mystery, and personally ac-
tivated through faith—that sets up the feedback
loop whereby even in the midst of overwhelming
oppositionality and despair, we can still set our
sights on and draw sustaining energy from that pole
star of Christ-Omega "*in quo omnia constant,*" as Teilhard's most cherished scriptural citation would have
it: "in whom all things hold together."

Perhaps this is what Teilhard means by "harnessing the energy of love." In our own times, it is surely
our best shot—perhaps our *only* shot—for doing
something that does not merely compound the
darkness. Teilhard's conviction that faith is not
something that we *have* but something that we *do* is
perhaps the best antidote possible to the despair and
distrust that paralyze so much of our post-modern

moral resolve. It is a call to step out of the boat onto the ocean of love, and discover—all our fear and skepticism to the contrary—that the water really *does* hold us up.

~May 2, 2017
The Omega Center at omegacenter.info

ABORTION AND
THE GREATER LIFE

PART I:
"A SURPRISING ECUMENISM..."

Both my spirits and my hopes have been raised by
the recent appearance of an important and already
game-changing new article in the most recent edi-
tion of *La Civilta Cattolica*. This is a prestigious Jesuit
publication, whose contents are personally vetted by
the Vatican Secretary of State and which can thus be
seen as a bellwether if not a *de facto* mouthpiece for
papal policy. Entitled "Evangelical Fundamentalism
and Catholic Integralism in the USA: A Surprising
Ecumenism", the article is the first attempt I have
seen to drive a significant intellectual wedge into the
murky moral alliance between conservative Catholi-

cism and Protestant evangelical fundamentalism that helped to catapult Donald Trump into office and is still a cornerstone of his support.

In this learned yet accessible study, co-authors Antonio Spadaro and Marcelo Figueroa (a Roman Catholic and a Presbyterian pastor, both of them respected editors and close friends of the Pope) trace the rise of Protestant Fundamentalism in the early 20th century, exploring its major doctrinal assertions and detailing its increasing infiltration into American politics. They conclude with a pointblank rejection of these doctrinal claims as antithetical and dangerous to authentic Catholic belief. The article's "blockbuster" assertion (understandably receiving wide play in the social media) is that *there is basically no ideological difference between fundamentalist Christianity and fundamentalist Islam*: both draw their juice from an identical "cult of an apocalypse," featuring a final confrontation between good ("us") and evil ("them") which will destroy the planet as we know it and usher in the reign of God.

The article represents a significant intellectual milestone and augurs a significant potential wind-shift in Vatican political activism. It's well worth some close study and discussion in our Wisdom circles. Over the next two or three blog-posts I'll share some of the reactions and implications it's been stirring up for me.

AN "ECUMENISM OF HATE"

While there are few surprises here for those already familiar with American religious history, the most welcome surprise is the message clearly being signaled that the Vatican is finally waking up to the theological implications of this "surprising" alliance that a significant segment of American Catholicism has been flirting with and is now taking a firm intellectual stance against its three constituent threads: the aforementioned "*cult of an apocalypse*," the "*prosperity gospel*" (which has deeply influenced several US presidents including our current one, Donald Trump), and a particularly distorted notion of *religious liberty* which sets the Church in permanent mortal combat with the presumed secularity of the state. The article powerfully calls the question on the present "ecumenism of hate," as the authors name it, and lays out in contrasting detail Pope Francis's vision of impartial and active engagement with the secular state in the hopes of securing a sustainable future for all humankind.

I applaud their work here because it lays a firm theological foundation for articulating the dangers implicit in the growing entanglement of the Catholic Church in American rightist politics. The article sets out clear standards by which, for example, self-styled über-Catholic Steve Bannon (specifically mentioned in the article) is in fact peddling a dangerously distorted version of Catholic teaching. It lays out clear benchmarks by which Catholics can sort through the confused rhetoric of evangelical fundamentalism and name its widening drift from classic Catholic doctrine. While the authors could have done more to clarify that evangelical fundamentalism represents a perversion of *Protestantism* as much as of Catholicism (not merely another of Protestantism's myriad confusing expressions), their analysis is nonetheless a solid intellectual milestone. It is also reflective of the Pope's strategic way of thinking: his preference for first building a solid theological and historical foundation for reflection and action, rather than simply leaping in with rhetorical or knee-jerk responses.

BUT THE ELEPHANT IN THE ROOM REMAINS…

While I am deeply gratified for the breakthrough this article represents, I must say that I find it naïve to expect that it will shift a single stone in the present Catholic/fundamentalist political alliance. The article mounts a strong case *theologically*, but in a glaring omission it manages to overlook the crucial point on which any practical consequences turn—namely, that the real basis for the alliance is not theological but *strategic.* Nor is this merely a minority dalliance, to be laid at the doorstep of a small subset of Catholic ultraconservatives; it represents the united "bottom line" of the Roman Catholic Church in America: the vast majority of its bishops, seminaries, and the message percolating into the parishes. *The real root of this alliance lies in the Roman Catholic Church's continuing fixation on the abortion issue,* together with this issue's now vigorously reemerging sidekick, *birth control.* This is the practical motivation behind the devil's pact with fundamentalism; if it takes casting one's lot with a "cult of the apocalypse" to ensure that *Roe versus Wade* is legally overturned, well, that's the unfortunate cost of doing business.

It seems unfortunate that in an article otherwise so thorough and scholarly, this rather sizable elephant in the room escapes mention. The article thus creates the impression that all we have to do is wake up to the theological errors inherent in the alliance with Protestant fundamentalism, and Catholics will come streaking back to a more inclusive and life-affirming version of the gospel. Well, maybe. But if you think this translates into any significant flipping of the Catholic vote in 2018, don't hold your breath.

To their credit, I am not sure that from the European (or even South American) perspective, the Vatican can really understand the ferocity with which the abortion issue has enthralled the popular American Catholic imagination. It's a quintessentially American stew, comprised in equal doses of high idealism and sentimentality run amuck. One need only to drive the interstate almost anywhere in the American South or Midwest and see the fully emblazoned billboards with a flat-lining EKG announcing "Abortion Stops a Beating Heart" to begin to appreciate the pungent mix of sentiment and sentimentality that makes this particular issue such a moral flashpoint. I personally know many Catholics (perhaps even the majority of my Catholic acquaintances) who, although good, solid, thoughtful people, not otherwise inclined toward hysteria, feel so strongly that this issue is so essential to their practice of Catholicism—and so underrepresented by any other advocacy group—that they will reluctantly sacrifice the entire rest of the gospel's "pro- life" teaching (as it might apply to immigrants, Muslims, accessible medical care, gun control, capital punishment) in order to secure this one point. It is this "unholy alliance" that really has provided the undefended back gateway——in fact, *sluiceway*—by which unethical politicians can continue to occupy their seats in congress, pawns in a game whose real movers and shakers are in fact the Ayn Rand-style kleptocrats (such as Paul Ryan, The Koch brothers, the Trump dynasty) or apocalyptic Armageddon-mongers such as Steve Bannon.

My continuing hope—which I have alluded to in articles and posts before—is that our brilliant and committed Pope will move increasingly in the direction of giving issue-specific theological guidance and direction to begin to disentangle this Gordian knot in a way that is both respectful of Catholic tradition and profoundly responsive to the desperate need of our one planet, trembling on the brink of environmental and social collapse.

In the face of this unprecedented global crisis, it is not enough merely to name and proclaim the ways in which the resurgence of Christian fundamentalism represents a perversion of Catholic doctrine. It is not enough merely to repeatedly denounce those currents in American politics fueling radical isolationism and environmental irresponsibility. It is not enough simply to continue to decry the Muslim ban, or lament the moral corruption of our present executive and congressional branches. These stances are all good insofar as they go. But we need to connect the dots. What is *really* needed—and comprises, I believe, the *real* Catholic moral priority of our time—is to develop specific guidelines for faithful Catholics clarifying how, when push comes to shove, to weigh priorities and make those difficult trade-offs so that abortion does not become the tail wagging an increasingly rabid and dangerous dog.

I am not a moral theologian—or even a Catholic for that matter—so I recognize that I will have no standing in that particular conversation. But as a

Christian Wisdom teacher and a concerned planetary citizen, I know that it is important for this conversation to be taking place and for imaginative new thinking to be invited from all quarters. Deliberations on this all-important topic so far left in the hands of the Catholic experts have yielded us no appreciable results, they've merely solidified the impasse. This is a human dilemma, and it is as a human family that we will solve it.

And so I propose here to engage this conversation among our Wisdom Community, asking us all, from our collective data banks of spiritual insight and life expertise, to engage this crucial impasse and see if the act of intelligent conversation can itself generate a bit of third force.

Over the next two or three blogs I will attempt, first of all, to lay out a potential pathway toward a new social contract with regard to the abortion issue. A pathway which, though admittedly a compromise, might be one that both Catholics and non-Catholics could live with. In the following, more extended blog, I will reflect on what light the Wisdom tradition has to shed on the beginnings of life and the nature of the soul, both key components in the present gridlock.

A good start has been made in this article, and I

commend it to you all for deeper study and reflection. But in accepting its conclusion that joining forces with a distorted Christian fundamentalism is not an option, the next step is to move courageously to confront the "root of the root" of this nefarious allegiance and speak directly of—*to*—the elephant in the room.

~July 17, 2017
Northeast Wisdom at northeastwisdom.org

ABORTION AND
THE GREATER LIFE

PART II: ABORTION, PRO-LIFE,
AND THE SECULAR STATE:
A MODEST PROPOSAL

In Part I of this series "A Surprising Ecumenism…" I invited members of our Wisdom Community to begin to engage a conversation on the emotion-charged issue of abortion rights as a means to promote respectful dialogue to think beyond this singular issue. It is with no little "fear and trembling" that I launch a foray into this quintessentially Catholic moral ground. But to the extent that abortion has become the tail wagging the dog, chaining much of the Catholic political conscience to the decidedly un-Christian agendas of the religious right—and to the extent that this "elephant in the room" continues to go unmentioned in the otherwise compelling moral analysis recently emerging from Vatican—I feel some obligation as an American citizen and a Wisdom teacher to at least try to get the ball rolling.

Forgive me: This is a long series. But take it in small doses, and take your time.

SOME PRELIMINARY REMARKS

If my memory serves me correctly, in one of his earliest encyclicals the Pope already laid out some firm groundwork here when he warned against a myopic, single-point focus that inevitably twists moral issues out of context. That's surely what the abortion issue has become in the US, an instantaneous flashpoint. But minus specific guidance as to how to back the Church down off this ledge, I don't see a practical way to take the first step toward defusing the tension. Is anybody seriously going to be damned fool enough to say, "Hey, we've decided that human life *doesn't* begin at conception," or "The rights of the unborn don't matter." There seems to be "no way to get from *he-ah* to *they-ah*," as we like to say in Maine, so the issue keeps running in circles.

SOME PRELIMINARY REFLECTIONS

Well-nigh universally, the liminal zones bordering life and death—i.e., what happens before birth or after death—have been regarded as a Mystery entrusted to the great spiritual traditions. The traditions offer different perspectives and instructions, but always with a common baseline of: 1) *respect* for the sacredness of these passages, and 2) the need to *prepare* for these passages, and to live one's life in *conscious relationship* with them. The plethora of spiritual practices offered by all sacred traditions are aimed, among other things, at developing a capacity to navigate this territory using more subtle and refined faculties of perception. (In Christian tradition this has traditionally been referred to as "faith.")

Across the board, the experience of most committed practitioners is that they eventually "live into" an intimate mystical familiarity with these liminal zones, acquiring the capacity to personally validate spiritual truths inaccessible by the rational intellect alone. Apart from this special training, the rational intellect remains dominant and is the basis of our common social contract. And this, I would say, is a good thing, for the attempt to impose theological dogma concerning the liminal when the inner faculties have not been yet developed to personally validate it leads to the devolution of faith into "blind faith" and opens the doors to theocratic totalitarianism and manifold forms of spiritual abuse to which our culture has become increasingly sensitized.

In former eras, when the population of any given nation was overwhelmingly of the same spiritual tradition, it was fairly simple to conflate these two tracks. The word "catholic" (as in "Catholic church") literally means "universal," and back in the era when the foundations of moral theology were being drawn, the known world was indeed just that. There were Catholics, "heathens," and missionaries: not much in between.

Nowadays, that is no longer even remotely true. Even in our tiniest nations—and certainly in a nation as vast and sprawling as the United States— there is no longer a single presumed overarching spiritual tradition. There are many—and increasingly *none*. The fragile glue maintaining civility across increasingly diverse populations is the social contract itself. "Co-exist" is indeed the watchword of our times. Any attempt by one group to reassert its claim that its vision is truly "catholic"—i.e. universally binding—inflicts inevitable misery and violence on the rest.

For this reason, I would propose to offer here what amounts to an essentially two-tier solution governing our deliberations on the abortion issue. The first tier (which one might argue is actually the more "catholic" in the original sense of the term) is consistent with our evolving understanding of human rights and our growing awareness, in a converging world, of the need for our common human family to set universal baselines for sustainable "best practices" with regard to environmental protection, resource allocation, disease control, and population control. The second tier, encapsulating the Wisdom carried in the sacred traditions, bears witness to the sacred potential of human life to come to its full spiritual fruition.

I will argue here that this "second tier" Wisdom, regardless of the tradition from which it emanates, is binding *within* that tradition, not *beyond* it. But within it, lived with fidelity and depth, it has the capacity— indeed, inevitably *will*—serve to redeem and purify the rather clumsier practice lived at the common level.

So here is my six-point proposal. This is clearly– –to my mind at least—simply an opening gambit that perhaps opens up a new way of framing the impasse. I eagerly invite your comments and re- finements. For the moment, I am thinking of this solely in terms of the USA, but hopefully it might have some eventual broader applications as well.

THE FIRST TIER (*the basic social contract*)

1. We agree that it will be the government's sacred responsibility to provide for the "life, liberty, and pursuit of happiness" of each of its citizens.

This is the classic social contract built into the foundations of our nation, and for 241 years it has served us well.

2. We agree that included among the fundamental rights implicit within these freedoms is the right for a woman to control her own body and to hold the decisive vote as to whether a new life will be formed within her body.

I know that this one will feel like a punch in the gut to those whose sense of moral duty has been firmly pinned in championing the rights of the unborn. But it is the logical and necessary consequence of Point 1, which is in turn the necessary starting point for a social contract founded on a clear separation of church and state. While the government will do its best to provide for the rights of *all* its citizens—including those *in utero*—nevertheless, in those difficult circumstances when the two are in direct conflict, we agree that the *rights of the present and quantifiable members of its citizenry take precedence over the rights of those still under the custody of the liminal sphere.*

But we have not thereby disposed of all concern for the unborn! For those feeling punched in the gut, please continue on to point 4.

3. We agree that in a world so deeply threatened by poverty, disease, and overpopulation, that the governmnt should exercise responsible stewardship by providing access to birth control and family planning.

These are envisioned not as moral concessions but as *fundamental health rights.*

This, then, would comprise my version of a sustainable social contract, with strong legal and moral precedent in the American notion of individual freedom.

THE SECOND TIER

4. We agree that the spiritual traditions are individually at liberty to invite or impose a higher standard of conduct upon their adherents in accordance with that tradition's understanding of moral and ethical obligation.

While this may at first sound like a double standard, I believe it is one where there is already strong precedent in the spiritual traditions. Already in Catholicism, for example (in fact, in all sacred traditions featuring a monastic expression), *marriage* is seen as the general baseline while *celibacy* is seen as a "higher way." The decision to walk the celibate path is not universally imposed, but on those who choose it, it becomes morally binding.

Traditionally the inducements offered to invite this higher level of commitment were pitched around *personal* fulfillment or excellence: a higher spiritual attainment, admission to heaven, etc. But as the Wisdom tradition has consistently maintained (and as modern physics, specifically the concept of quantum entanglement, confirms), *the real efficacy of this higher level of practice lies in its leavening effect upon the whole*, raising the bar of spiritual energy and available grace for everyone. A spiritual path practiced with high integrity and commitment emits a transforming energy of its own, which goes much further in actually securing a higher level of spiritual understanding than individuals conscripted into a level of moral behavior they neither understand nor personally assent to.

My intuition is that a significant portion of Catholics voluntarily taking on the Church's traditional moral teachings on family planning and abortion would do more to better the lot of the unborn than an entire nation forced into compliance with laws experienced as coercive and personally injurious. If the active practice of an authentic sacred tradition produces as its fruits "peace, patience, kindness, goodness, faithfulness, gentleness, and self-control," as Christian tradition (and all traditions) have staunchly maintained, then it is to be expected that these qualities, *once actually attained*, would percolate through the entire body of our country's citizenry, if nothing else elevating the climate and respectfulness of the civic discourse. It has always been said that Christians taught first by example—by the fragrance of a life lived with compassionate integrity. It is still our best bet going into the future, particularly where the changes we're looking to see involve those liminal realms—birth and death—where the spiritual integrity of the gesture is far more impactful than the immediate victory wrested by means which belie their ends.

The last two points are more general, extending beyond the specific abortion issue in order to attempt to establish a climate in which a pluralistic nation, in rapid social transition and spanning at least a three-level gap in levels of consciousness as measured by contemporary evolutionary maps (from amber to green, tribal to world-centric), might still continue to engage in civil discourse and a healthy give-and-take:

> *5. We agree that government will not intervene with the internal standards of conduct imposed by a spiritual tradition upon its adherents, so long as these standards do not directly threaten the public health or safety. Neither will it establish and promote these standards as binding upon all its citizens.*

I would expect this to be a continuing grey area––and rightly so—in that ongoing dance between religious freedom and public safety. There will still be regular legal challenges—as to, for example, whether

Christian Scientists should be compelled to seek medical attention for their children or Old Order Mennonites forbidden to use corporal punishment on theirs; whether homophobic town clerks should be required to issue marriage licenses to gay couples or homophobic merchants be required to bake them wedding cakes. In a less polarized society than ours has now become, this would all remain within the realm of healthy give-and-take by which the collective social conscience is slowly nudged ahead.

In order to back down the polarization, however, which by now has escalated to unmanageable levels, I would add in a corollary here which, while it personally breaks my liberal heart, is I believe the only realistic concession that will represent a significant stance of "bargaining in good faith" to ease the present stand-off:

> *5a: The government agrees not to use its juridical power to impose secular affirmative action standards upon dissenting spiritual groups operating within their own sectarian networks.*

In this matter, I am much guided by the model set by my own Episcopal Church in its landmark decisions to embrace women's ordination and gay marriage. While these decisions, once passed by the General Convention, became the law of the Church, there was a long timeline for total compliance, and wide latitude was given for dissenting clergy and congregations to slowly acclimatize to the new state of affairs through continued conversation and study, with the right to personally opt out of participation in actions that felt to them morally offensive (bishops opposed to women's ordination, for example, would be able to place their women postulants under the care of a neighboring bishop, nor would a church adamantly uncomfortable with women priests have one foisted upon them). Time was allowed for healing and assimilation, with responses erring on the side of forbearance rather than a self-righteous pressing of the issue.

> *6. Spiritual groups will refrain from seeking to impose their specific moral values or agenda as the law of the land, to the extent that these values either exceed or undercut baseline freedoms already guaranteed above.*

A WORK IN PROGRESS….

The proposal set forth here is admittedly a compromise. But beyond perhaps easing the polarization, I believe it actually restores a generically rightful balance. In arguing that *sacred teachings are binding within a specific spiritual tradition but not beyond it*, I believe I am not only acknowledging one of the realities of our pluralistic world, but actually calling on an inherent capacity of these two complimentary streams to counterbalance and bootstrap each other. At its best, the secular state can rescue the sacred traditions from their tendency toward monological thinking and extremism. And at their best, the sacred traditions remind us that the meaning of life is derived from exactly those liminal edges, in the renewed and deeper stabilization of the capacity to live as human beings according to those higher faculties of perception which have never been fully actualized—and by my estimation *never* will—within purely secular models. Severally and collectively, the spiritual traditions are the evolutionary omega, calling us on to what we have forgotten, or what we may still become.

I realize that many of my Catholic friends will be saying, "yes, but what about all those unborn babies?" As you recall, this proposal began with two assertions, both emerging from my perspective as Wisdom teacher. The first is that *pre-birth* and *post-death* belong to those great liminal Mysteries of life, and are best left in the custody of the sacred traditions; the second is that the spiritual practices carefully curated by each of these traditions afford access to these Mysteries in ways that the rational mind cannot comprehend. In the absence of this specific spiritual training (in Christianity, its lineage flows through contemplative prayer), *perception will default to the rational mind*, where abortion indeed looks like "baby killing," and emotions instantly bridle at this presumed assault on the innocent. From the more rounded, three-dimensional perspective that opens up from the "mind in the heart," the situation takes on an entirely different coloration. It is this Wisdom perspective that I will be exploring as this series moves towards its conclusion.

~July 25, 2017
Northeast Wisdom at northeastwisdom.org

ABORTION AND
THE GREATER LIFE

PART III:
WHEN DOES "LIFE" BEGIN?

In this third part of what is a seven-part series, I hope to bring a Wisdom perspective to that profound liminal sphere encompassing conception, birth, and the formation of the soul. For it's in the metaphysical confusion surrounding these mysteries, I believe, that the roots of our present abortion conundrum really have their origin.

Note that I say "a Wisdom perspective" rather that "the Wisdom perspective," for the Wisdom tradition is by no means monochrome. My comments here reflect the strands of the lineage that have most directly informed my own understanding, specifically, the Gurdjieff Work and the Christian mystical/esoteric lineage running through the Gos-

pel of Thomas, the Philokalia, Jacob Boehme, and Pierre Teilhard de Chardin. They also reflect some of the thinking at the forefront of contemporary embryology, particularly as represented in the work of Dutch embryologist Jaap van der Wal.

THE BEGINNINGS OF LIFE

The Wisdom tradition would affirm vigorously that life does not merely begin at conception; it is *already well underway* by the time of conception, "life" here understood not as a purely biological phenomenon, but *as flow, dynamism, and intelligent purposiveness*. In contrast to earlier, more mechanical models, which tended to see conception in Darwinian terms ("the fittest sperm takes the egg"), contemporary embryological research suggests a much more collaborative model, far more akin to Nashian Game Theory than to Darwinian survival of the fittest. A myriad of sperm collaborate to place a *single* sperm before the egg, which then *opens*—volitionally—rather than simply being battered or overwhelmed.

There is evidence as well that conception occurs according to a full-fledged Law of Three model. It's not simply sperm/egg//baby, but rather, sperm/egg/X//baby, where X represents the infusion of some mysterious animating force beyond the immediate biochemistry.

Those of us who participated in the 2012 Tucson Wisdom School will no doubt never forget that powerful moment when Wisdom student Nancy Denman, a research embryologist from British Columbia, described how the process of conception actually occurs:

> *"The egg opens to a single sperm," she explained, "then closes. For about twenty-four hours there is stillness. Then all of a sudden, the egg starts vibrating violently. 'Ignition!!!' we all call it."*
>
> *Then she added parenthetically, "Those of us of a more religious bent might be inclined to describe it as "the descent of the Spirit."*

However, this X-factor is named, it certainly seems to function as a third term in the old "nature versus nurture" conundrum, offering still another line of explanation as to why babies conceived by the same parents and raised in the same household under the same value system frequently wind up displaying such markedly different personality traits. "Our essence comes from the stars," Gurdjieff always insisted. There is something in the formation of a new life that cannot be reduced to pure biochemistry; it seems to be an emergent property of the act of conception itself.

LIFE NOT SOUL

So far so good. There is nothing in the above that should raise any eyebrows whatsoever among even the most ardent pro-lifers. "What part of *life* do you not understand?" If anything, we are pushing back the leading edge of life in to even earlier in the process, in to the intrinsic purposiveness that Teilhard de Chardin and others would see as part of the irreversible intelligence of evolution itself.

But hang onto your hats; this next step is where we are about to part company rather dramatically with traditional pro-life metaphysics. For the Wisdom tradition would suggest that *life*—which indubitably is present at the moment of conception if not well before—is not synonymous with *Soul*. The terms are often used interchangeably, and it is precisely here, in this confusion, that the Gordian knot is originally tied.

In traditional Catholic metaphysics, this "x-factor" would immediately be identified as "the soul," the essence of the living human being. The soul is created by God and bestowed at conception. Once bestowed, it is henceforward immortal within the cosmos; death will change its state but will not destroy it. Thus, the soul trajectory is established from the very beginning; from this the moment of conception forward, this uniquely particular and fully formed human identity will make its way through the journey of life, along the way accumulating virtue or vice—in acknowledgement of which, it will be assigned its permanent dwelling place in either heaven or hell.

In the light of this venerable but antiquated metaphysical roadmap (note how it's steeped in "substance theology," long since invalidated by contemporary scientific models), it is easy to understand both the urgency and the pathos dominating the "pro-life" strategy. Denying the gift of life to even a two-cell fetus is tantamount to killing a defenseless human soul. The assumption governing much of the pro-life rhetoric seems to be that somehow pro-choice folks don't "get" that a human life is a human soul and need to be shown that it is, often in emotionally exaggerated and manipulative ways. Hence those "abortion stops a beating heart" billboards.

The Wisdom tradition—at least the lineage of the tradition I have been formed in—would see it differently. What is bestowed in that moment of "ignition" is not yet a soul, but rather, *the potential to develop a soul*. Soul does not come at the beginning; it comes at the end, forged and fused in the crucible of life itself (or perhaps better, in the *womb* of life) through the conscious weaving of that hand which is dealt at the moment of conception.

The notion of a "*developmental soul*" comes as a shock and perhaps even an affront to traditional

Christian metaphysics. But hear me out here; it has been a staple in the Western esoteric tradition from the get-go, as I will document in "Part IV: The Developmental Soul." But even more compellingly, it holds the potential, I believe, to bring an authentic resolution to the abortion impasse, and to tie together that great desideratum so far escaping us: that integral "pro-life" stance that sees *all* stages of life as equally compelling and worthy of sacred protection.

~*August 21, 2017*
Northeast Wisdom at northeastwisdom.org

ABORTION AND
THE GREATER LIFE

PART IV:
THE DEVELOPMENTAL SOUL

ESSENCE

According to Gurdjieff, the mysterious "x-factor" that enters in the moment of conception is not yet soul but *essence*. Think of it as the hand of cards you're dealt at the start of a card game. It comprises a set of unique characteristics, including race, gender (and most likely gender orientation), basic body type and other genetic factors, influences emerging from more distant ancestry and bloodline—and yes, that unquantifiable legacy "from the stars"—all combined primarily according to what Teilhard would call "*tatonnement*" ("trial and error"): evolution's predilection for trying out any and all possibilities. Cumulatively, all of the above will combine to confer on you what is commonly known as your "nature."

Notice how there is no need to stipulate an "artist" God here, specifically designing a unique human being; what's being pictured here is simply a lawful playing out of a freedom already inherent within Creation itself. Essence is not customized, not micro-managed—at least according to most schools of inner work I'm familiar with. That may take some getting used to, and for those of you finding yourself already in resistance mode, I encourage you simply to let this new perspective settle in a bit. Rest assured that I do intend to talk about the origin of the personal in due course.

Once formed, essence will take its place as one of the three constituent terms in an ongoing *dynamism of becoming* which, not surprisingly, will play out according to the Law of Three. The other two terms, according to modern Sufi master Kabir Helminski (who reflects this same Wisdom lineage that I myself was trained in), are *spirit* and *heart*.

Spirit is that ever-roving, unboundaried, invisible divine dancing partner, participating in every movement of our life according to its own deepest teleology, namely, self-disclosure (remember "*I was a hidden treasure and I longed to be known*"?). It generally plays the role of first force, Holy Affirming: ever prodding, nudging, unfolding.

Essence will typically play the role of Holy Denying, the "bloc résistant" in which Spirit will reveal its face. Through its very *embodied finitude* essence provides both the necessary raw material and the necessary friction to allow the pure movement of spirit to reveal itself in time and form.

Heart—or *conscience*—is the alchemical "third term" that is catalyzed in us through a life lived in growing consciousness, authenticity, obedience (as in *ob-audire*, "listen from the depths"), and that active cultivation of the self-reflective potential miraculously gifted to human consciousness. Heart is the unique fruit of a life wisely and fully engaged. More important, from the perspective of the roadmap I'm laying out here, it contributes the crucial third force, or "holy reconciling," which makes possible that ultimate desideratum, namely, the fully arisen *soul*. Soul (or as Helminski calls it, "the essential self") is precisely that "fourth in a new dimension" which arises out of conscious weaving of those other three—spirit, essence, and heart—within the great womb of life.

While this statement may sound jarring, note how it is already well embedded in early Christian tradition. The Gospel of Thomas puts it as starkly as possible in logion 70: "If you bring forth what is within you, that which you bring forth will save you. If you fail to bring forth that which is within you, that which you fail to bring forth will destroy you." "*That which is within you*" is your embryonic soul.

Jesus seems to be reinforcing this teaching in his celebrated parable of the talents—once you recognize, of course, that the "talents" are not our aptitudes and gifts (which belong to essence), but rather, *these soul potentialities transformed and quickened in the light of conscience/heart.* This message comes through powerfully as well in the medieval mystic Jacob Boehme; it is in fact the driveshaft of his entire metaphysics. But it peers out as well from any number of other Christian mystics, even those of much more theoretically "traditional" metaphysical training and temperaments. One of the most powerful statements of this principle I know comes in contemporary Jesuit Ladislaus Boros' spiritual classic, *The Mystery of Death*:

> *From the facts of existence and the surrounding world an inner sphere of being a human is built up. This inner man is brought about by a never-ending (conscious) daily application, on the treadmill of duties, annoyances, joys and difficulties. From these insignificant actions freely performed, the decisive freedom is built up—freedom from oneself, freedom to view one's own existence from outside... From the crowded days and years of joy and sorrow something has crystallized out, the rudimentary forms of which were already present in all his experiences, his struggle, his creative work, his patience and love—namely, the inner self, the*

108

individual, supremely individual creation of a man. He has given his own shape to the determinisms of life by a daily conquest of them; he has become master of the multiple relationships that go to make him up by accepting them as the raw materials *(emphasis mine) of his self. Now he begins to "be." (pp 60 -61)*

As far as I know, Boros never directly encountered the Christian Inner tradition, let alone the teachings of the Asian spiritual traditions. Yet he has eloquently described here what would be easily recognizable in any of these other streams as "Witnessing Self." He has captured precisely the same nuance articulated by *The Gospel of Thomas*, Boehme, Gurdjieff, and Jacob Needleman—namely, that our "soul" is not our raw essence per se, but something of an entirely different nature which is alchemized *through the active engagement of essence with heart/consciousness*. It is not so much a *substance* (at least in terms of corporeality as we understand it in this life) but more a *process*—or as Jacob Boeheme had it, a *tincture*, a quality of our essential aliveness which shines through the lineaments of this life like a shaft of imperishable light. Above all, it is not conferred at the start, but brought into being *in this life* through the quality of our conscious work.

Within the western Wisdom tradition this imperishable "other" is sometimes known as "*second body*" or "*the wedding garment*." Actualizing it is seen—with some urgency—as the real business of our earthly sojourn.

Admittedly, there is a hard edge to this teaching, jolting us into responsible stewardship of our own time in human consciousness. We can choose, if we like, to drift downstream on the currents of pain or pleasure. We can invest our whole life energy worshipping the golden calf of ego. Or we can get with the cosmic program and come to grips with the real purpose of our time here as we humbly acknowledge that soul is not an automatic birthright, but rather, *the final alchemy of a life lived here in conscious alignment with higher cosmic purposes.*

Furthermore, the tradition states—essentially unequivocally—that this second body, or wedding garment, must be formed in *this* life. That is why it is called a wedding garment: because it is the appropriate and necessary regalia for the "wedding banquet" of eternal life—which, incidentally, does not begin *after* we leave this body, but here and now as this new substantiality we bear within us increasingly allows us to perceive, that the gates of heaven are, truly, everywhere.

This is soulwork in the true sense of the term:

not the "soft" version that passes for soulwork to-day, preoccupied with unraveling dreams and deciphering messages from our "inner guides," but the adamantine work of bringing something into existence here that will have coherence and substantiality beyond just this realm. Gurdjieff called it our "Real I."

"You must find that in you that already lives beyond death and begin to live out of it now," my teacher Rafe taught me, encapsulating the essence of this teaching in his own plain words. To defer this project till after we die is too late; for in, as Jacob Boehme bluntly puts it, "everything lies where it has fallen." This is not, by the way, a question of "final judgment," of some higher being deciding you are "unworthy." It's simply that the conditions in the next realm out, sometimes known as the Imaginal, are finer and drawn to far closer tolerances than in this life. Only something of a similar fineness will pass through the sieve.

I am theologian enough to know that the immediate argument conventionally trained Christians will raise against this is that it seems to defy the promise of Psalm 139—"Before I formed you in the womb I knew you"—and replace the intimate and personal nature of our lifelong human relationship with God with an impersonal and even harsh algorithm. I do not believe this is actually so. I will have more to say about the personal in "Part V: Teilhard, The Personal and the Developmental Soul," with the intuition that this alternative vision, certainly strongly intimated by Jesus, is actually far more merciful and cosmically ennobling.

The second objection, of course, is that this sounds like a classic recipe for spiritual materialism. (I can already picture the internet ads for second-body-building nutritional supplements and "wedding garment" consultants! But the checks and balances factor, built right into this equation, lies in the fact that the requisite food for building second body is, in Gurdjieff's famous formula, "conscious labor and intentional suffering." Second body cannot be attained through self-maximization, but only through the classic route variously known in the sacred traditions as *kenosis* and humility. "We ascend by descending," as the Rule of St. Benedict succinctly observes. There is no other way.

For those who opt out, preferring to live out their days in their egoic comfort zone (a condition known in the Inner tradition in as "sleep"), the potentiality offered at birth to become a soul is simply returned, stillborn. Nothing has germinated here of permanent substantiality; nothing has become viable beyond the womb of this life. Such existences, in Gurdjieff's words, become "food for the moon." At death their temporary selfhood dissolves back into its original physical components and takes its small part in the vast network of reciprocal feeding, by which the cosmos bootstraps itself. Nothing is finally wasted.

From the Work perspective, then, abortion is not something that befalls merely a fetus. It happens at *all* stages, and is in fact the tragic outcome of most human lives. Lulled into complacency by the illusion that we already "have" souls, we fail to engage the real task of spiritual germination and wind up dreaming our lives away.

Only when this inconvenient truth is finally, fully faced will the real question of what it means to be "pro-life" find its authentic balance.

~August 27, 2017
Northeast Wisdom at northeastwisdom.org

ABORTION AND
THE GREATER LIFE

PART V:
TEILHARD, THE PERSONAL,
AND THE DEVELOPMENTAL SOUL

But what about psalm 139?

The biggest challenge in wrapping one's head around this Wisdom notion of a developmental soul—at least for traditionally reared religious folks—is that it seems to fly in the face of that well-loved Biblical assurance that God is personally and intimately invested in the creation of each and every human being. "For you yourself created my inmost parts; you knit me together in my mother's womb," the psalm text assures. In the face of this apparently

114

explicit assurance that each human soul originates in God and reflects God's personal handiwork, the alternative version—that developing a soul is the principal business of this life and that not all human lives will get there—seems bleak and impersonal. What could possibly be the advantage of looking at things this way?

The advantage is that it might—just *might*—knock us out of a *cul-de-sac* of sloppy and sentimental thinking based on an antiquated metaphysics that is no longer supported by science.

There is a strong tendency to use the terms "life," "soul," and "human person" interchangeably, as if they are equivalent. They manifestly are *not*. "Life begins at conception," some of you have passionately reiterated—but not so; according to contemporary scientific models; *life is already well underway at the time of conception*; it is a property already shared by sperm and egg since it belongs as a general condition to the biosphere. Nor is the *soul* created at conception, if the developmental roadmap is to be taken seriously; soul is the fruit of the journey, not the seed.

What is created in that "ignition" moment at conception—and yes, it is a pivotal moment—is the *individual human life*, the temporarily separated spark of divine consciousness that will have the option, with tenacity and luck, to return to the divine fullness having realized a very different kind of substantiality within the cosmos.

The Wisdom teaching is clear: below a certain threshold death brings an end to this temporary sense of individuated selfhood. The "soul" is not destroyed (since it has not yet come into being in the first place); the individual essence components are simply reabsorbed back into the biosphere. As Jesus himself expresses this ancient teaching in the Gospel of Mary Magdalene:

> *All of nature with its forms and creatures exist together and are interwoven with each other. They will be resolved back, however, to their own proper origin, for the compositions of matter return to the original roots of their nature...*

Above this threshold—with the crystallization of what we have been calling "second body" or *soul* in the true esoteric sense of the term, this dissolution does not take place (not immediately, at any rate). The individuality thus formed as the fruit of "conscious labor and intentional suffering" can hold his or her personhood within a wider spiritual cosmos which is not affected by the dissolution of the physical (earth-plane) body. This attainment is always viewed as being for cosmic servanthood, not for personal glory.

TEILHARD AND THE PERSONAL

Interestingly, Teilhard de Chardin arrives at a remarkably similar assessment from his scientific perspective. There is indeed a dividing line, he feels, and it is integrally related to some threshold of consciousness crossed in the human species. As he writes with astonishing power toward the end of *The Human Phenomenon* (p. 194):

> *Certainly the human being appears to disintegrate just like the animal. But here and there the phenomenon functions in reverse. Through death in the animal the radial [energy] is reabsorbed into the tangential. In the human, the radial escapes the tangential and is freed from it. There is an escape from entropy by a sudden reversal toward Omega. Death itself is hominized. (1)*

Yes, the Wisdom tradition would agree. That is precisely what happens. But whereas Teilhard would, at first, appear to be according this "escape from the law of entropy" to *all* humans, the developmental model would assert that it in fact occurs to only *some* of them: those who, in the course of their lives have acquired/developed a soul—or, to put it in Teilhardian language, *who have passed from mere individuals to becoming persons.*

But is Teilhard in fact conferring this blessing on the entire human species? You have to admit, his "*but here and there*" is quite a teaser!

We know from elsewhere in *The Human Phenomenon*—and in fact, throughout his work—that Teilhard draws a very clear distinction between an individual and a *person*. For him the two terms are not synonymous, but more like *progressive stages* of a human journey. The "individual" is simply an autonomous human unit operating in accordance with biological necessity. The "person" has developed the gift of genuine interiority (in a way that dovetails closely with that Boros quote I shared with you in "Part IV: The Developmental Soul"). This interiority, moreover, is not individualistic or isolationist but is simultaneously the awareness of belonging to a greater whole. It is grounded in a dawning sense of a deeper human collectivity, which is at the same time a new evolutionary emergence.

The journey from individual to person is the essence of what Teilhard means by "hominization." If this key Teilhardian term is understood to designate not simply the evolutionary appearance of the species *homo sapiens*, but rather the interior journey within each member of this species as he or she moves toward becoming a person, then we have a model which is essentially in line with the great Wisdom lineage, of which Teilhard is our most recent powerful spokesperson.

"AN IMMENSE SOLICITUDE–
IN THE SPHERE OF THE PERSON...."

As a biologist, Teilhard knows only too well that the biosphere is characterized by an extravagant wastefulness. Living organisms come into being in astonishing profusion, only to vanish just as quickly. In a powerful philosophical reflection on "The Ways of Life," tucked into an early chapter in *The Human Phenomenon* he designates the three core characteristics of life as *profusion*, ingenuity, and *indifference toward individuals*:

> *So many times, art, poetry, and even philosophy have depicted nature like a woman, blindfolded, trampling down a dust of crushed existences. In life's profusion, we find the first traces of this apparent hardheartedness. Like Tolstoy's grasshoppers, life passes over a bridge of accumulated corpses... Life is more real than lives, as it has been said...*

> *Here lost in number. There torn apart in the collective... The dramatic and perpetual opposition in the course of evolution between the element born of the multiple and the multiple constantly being born in the element. (p. 67)*

Perhaps this perspective might be of some dark consolation as we step up to the plate and ponder the apparent "heartlessness" of a model in which many individualized essences, do indeed "spontaneously abort," failing to transform that initial individualized essence into a soul that will be cosmically viable beyond the womb of this life. This is, as Teilhard points out, simply the universal condition of the biosphere, and insofar as one remains firmly planted in that realm, its laws will continue to hold sway, no matter how hard we stamp our feet and emote about "personal" nature of each newly conceived human life. The individual is not yet the personal. That belongs to another sphere.

But, says Teilhard, the value we are obliquely intuiting here does in fact exist; we are simply looking for it in the wrong place; assigning it to the wrong level of consciousness:

> *Insofar as the general movement of life becomes more ordered, in spite of periodic resumptions of the offensive the conflict tends to resolve itself. Yet it is cruelly recognizable right the end. Only from the spirit, where it reaches its felt paroxysm, will the antimony clear; and the world's indifference to its elements be transformed into an immense solicitude—in the sphere of the person. (p. 67)*

"We are not there yet," he cautions. And yet he does hold out for us here a pathway of hope, and a way of potentially resolving the fierce impasse around the personal so categorically invested in the newly conceived fetus. By Teilhard's standards a fetus is a human individual, but it is not yet a person. And in tasting the difference between the two (and the developmental ground to be covered here which is the true meaning of being "pro-life"), we may finally be able to move forward.

~*September 3, 2017*
Northeast Wisdom at northeastwisdom.org

1. This passage is filled with Teilhard-speak; my apologies. Tangential energy is for him the physical energy routinely measured by science. Radial energy corresponds to what most esoteric maps would call "psychic" energy: the finer energy of consciousness as it expresses itself in attention, prayer, will, or, for Teilhard, increasing self-articulation and complexification. Omega is his evolutionary end-point, identical with Christ; "hominized" means transformed in the direction of becoming more fully human in its highest sense: coherent, conscious, compassionate.

ABORTION AND
THE GREATER LIFE

PART VI: FULLNESS OF LIFE:
A BRIEF POETIC INTERLUDE

The clear, simple truth: Nothing can fall out of God.

Where would it go?

God is not "*somebody*" (not me)—"*somewhere else*" (not here.) God is the *All*, the now, the whole; the undivided, dynamic totality of form and formlessness. As Barbara Brown Taylor pictures it so vibrantly in *The Luminous Web*:

> *Where is God in this picture? God is all over the place. God is up there, down here, inside my skin and out. God is the web, the energy, the space, the light—not captured in them, as if any of those concepts were more real than what unites them—but*

revealed in that singular, vast net of relationship
that animates everything that is. (p. 74)

We are pouring from fullness to fullness here.

From the perspective of the cove, the tide rises and falls in great contrasting cycles. A wharf riding gently at sea level on the high tide may be perched fifteen feet above a mudflat when the tide has emptied out. The sea ebbs and flows; the cove appears as "full" or "empty." But from the perspective of the ocean, the volume of water is always the same; like a great watery amoeba it simply extends and retracts its arms into the nooks and crannies of coastline from its own serenely undiminished magnitude.

When we think about life in terms of rising-and-falling, beginning-and-ending, we are betraying our finite perspective. "The individual drop that we are disappears in time," writes Raimon Panikkar in *Christophany* (p. 130). "But the personal water that we are (the drop's water) lives eternally—if, that is, we have succeeded in realizing the (divine) water that we are." If, in other words, if we have succeeded in shifting our perspective from cove to ocean.

It's not easy, for sure. Down here in earth-time, the fleetingness of duration weighs heavily on us. "The paths of glory lead but to the grave," Thomas Grey famously lamented. So brief the duration of a human life; so quickly over and gone. And when

123

that life is but embryonic, cut off before it is even born, the pathos seems doubly brutal. We feel it as an exception, a violation. We do not see—do not *want* to see—even the slightest continuity with the universal, impartial agency of those "Ways of Life" Teilhard speaks of–ingenuity, profusion, *indifference* (!!)—to which all lower orders in the chain of life are bound. Duration seems so precious to us when it comes to human beings; less so, perhaps when we try to extend it to virtual particles or stars exploding in-and-out of existence in distant galaxies—or for that matter, to the millions of ungerminated seeds for every fetus engendered; to the ants, viruses, butterflies, starfish washed up on a beach in a freak flood tide, abandoned pets, livestock en route to the slaughterhouse… Where do our hearts draw the line?

"Only from the spirit, where it reaches its *felt* paroxysm, will the antinomy clear," writes Teilhard––"and the world's indifference to its elements will be transformed into an immense solicitude—in the sphere of the person." But perhaps not quite in the way we are expecting. Personhood does not change the laws to which the entire created order is bound, but perhaps it gives us some perspective *by rescuing consciousness from its captivity to duration.*

So what about all those "souls" who don't get a chance to live this life, spread their wings, even draw their first breath? Is something unbearably precious lost forever? As I ponder, from my own human perspective, the pathos of a life seemingly cut short in time, I find myself drawn back time and again to this haunting poem by Laura Gilpin (entitled "The Two-headed Calf"), which I first came across in Belden Lane's spiritual classic, *The Solace of Fierce Landscapes*:

> *Tomorrow when the farm boys find this*
> *freak of nature, they will wrap his body*
> *in newspaper and carry him to the museum.*

> *But tonight he is alive in the north*
> *field with his mother. It is a perfect*
> *summer evening: the moon rising over*
> *the orchard, the wind in the grass.*
> *And as he stares into the sky; there are*
> *twice as many stars as usual.*

I offer this poem as a kind of dark solace in the face of that sickening, "punched-in-the-gut" feeling that arises whenever we try to fathom a life that will never know the grace of duration in time. All life is one life, ultimately, and this one life is in the hands of God and *is* the hands of God. As humans, we properly feel grief and immense pathos when a potential life trajectory is suddenly cut off, either intentionally or by accident, and it is right that we should; that is the nature of our human sentiency. But to the extent that we can open our hearts and learn to feel *all* of life—in all its myriad yet particular forms—as the seamless sentiency of God, then perhaps we can loosen our grip on individual duration and let the unbroken wholeness of life flow according to its own mysterious deeper rhythm. The antidote to hardness of heart (from which our culture certainly suffers) may not lie so much in exaggerating the rights of the unborn as in opening our hearts more deeply to the unity—and freefall—that is divine love.

Nothing can fall out of God. Each and every created essence—whether plant, mineral, animal, human—participates in the symphony of divine self-disclosure in its own way and knows the fullness of divine mercy according to its own mode of perceptivity. Even a stone. Even a blade of grass. Most certainly a fetus. Most certainly at the hour of our death. Duration does not affect that holographic fullness, presumably even in a virtual particle. Even––sometimes *especially*—in brevity, the intensity of the whole is conveyed in a heightened form—twice as many stars as usual!

Granted, the gift of time gives us the window of opportunity to do some pretty amazing stuff—like developing a soul, for one! But the soul is for cosmic service. Cosmic *fullness* is something else again. It is the free and gratuitous birthright bestowed by God on every quark and particle of the created order. And we get to participate in it freely, fully, here and now, simply because each one of us is a tiny shareholder in the divine aliveness. Nor does even an "interrupted life" ever pass out of the knowingness of God. "Before I formed you in the womb, I knew you," says Psalm 139—and if we turn that promise just slightly sideways, we can see in it a deeper assurance that may have slipped by us on the first pass. Each individualized life is a trajectory—*a probability wave*, quantum physicists would call it—of divine self-manifestation that already exists in the heart of God. The heart of God is the infinite abyss of all possibilities. Its time will come round again.

~September 8, 2017
Northeast Wisdom at northeastwisdom.org

ABORTION AND
THE GREATER LIFE

PART VII: HEALING THE
ELEPHANT IN THE WOMB

As we come down the home stretch in this extended Wisdom inquiry into the abortion issue, I've tried to draw together here some of the most important implications and "business arising" out this exploration. Most of my following "top five" have already been touched on in Part I - VI, but a few are new (though obviously following from points already raised).

Here we go:

1. REFRAMING

The whole conversation around the abortion issue needs to begin with a comprehensive reframing of the metaphysical assumptions on which it rests: away from a substance-theology-driven fixation on nailing down the precise moment when "life" begins (implicitly understood as meaning an individual human soul) and toward a wider appreciation of the entire life journey as a single, interwoven dynamism of "soul-making" in which each stage of the journey is equally vulnerable and precious. When does a daffodil become a daffodil? Is daffodil the bulb? The shoot? The bud? The flower? It is all of the above, yet none insofar as a stage is taken in isolation. In the traditional Wisdom maps—confirmed as well as in the more dynamic relational models emerging from the leading edges of biophysics and evolutionary theology—the term "pro-life" can no longer be usurped by any single phase of the journey, for *the soul is the fruit of the entire life journey*, not merely of the moment of conception.

This Wisdom understanding of "pro-life" assumes that the boundaries demarcating an individual life from the greater relational field that has supported its gestation/individuation—*and will continue to do so for the entire course of its life*—are always a bit indistinct, marked by considerable reciprocity at each step of the way. Attempting to establish identity by separating an individual element from the whole is an old, old metaphysical habit that no longer matches the shape of our dynamically interwoven universe. At every phase life makes its way juggling difficult balances and hard trade-offs. To be pro-life—not merely "pro-*birth*"—implies an acknowledgement of that challenging terrain and the willingness to bring forbearance and mercy to the entire unfolding.

2. COMPASSIONATE SPEAKING

As an important initial step in that direction, we need to become much more forbearing and merciful in our use of language. Precision is necessary—"soul," "life," and "individual essence" are *not* synonyms, and when used as if they are, they result in creating what Arthur Lovejoy once defined as *emotional pathos*–language wielded for sentimental and/or manipulative effect. Christianity is already vulnerable enough to that sort of emotional manipulation; it has been standard devotional and even theological practice for centuries. We need to tread extremely gently here, and to be doubly alert to well-worn rut tracks of associative thinking.

Above all, it seems to me that the word "murder" has no place in any helpful discussion of the abortion issue. Technically, yes, abortion terminates an incipient human life. But when connotation—not merely denotation—is factored in, murder typically implies malevolent intent; it *already presumes a crime.* (1) To impose this set of associations on a decision making process which virtually always unfolds in the realm of human anguish is inflammatory and cruel. Is it also murder to "put down" a pet? To withdraw life support from a loved one following a catastrophic stroke? Do these decisions—which also terminate a life—always presume malevolent intent?

At very most, we are speaking here of "fetal homicide." My own preference would be to recognize that in those great liminal zones surrounding birth and death, where life is not yet (or no longer) fully viable on its own, we need a whole different way of languaging those painful but sometimes necessary decisions to end the life of another sentient being. I am not suggesting euphemism here, but rather an honest and compassionate clarity that would serve the goal of healing—not simply anger and blame.

3. ACKNOWLEDGING THE SHADOW

That being said, abortion *does* end the life of another sentient being, and such a decision is never easy or pain-free. It inflicts deep wounds on the human psyche (I believe this is true even in the case of putting down a pet), and these wounds are long in healing and reverberate on many planes; in that sense, abortion is a karmic act. Because of the harm it invariably engenders (to self, fetus, relationship), it is never simply a medical "procedure," let alone a "normal" method of birth control. It should always be considered exceptional: a "least preferable" option to be invoked only after alternatives have been carefully weighed and rejected.

Since the clearly documented shadow side of abortion still tends to be under-acknowledged in pro-choice presentations, there seems to be an obvious need for a more balanced emphasis in sexual education, together with a concerted effort to make standard forms of contraception readily and blamelessly available: the only strategy to date that has yielded a conclusive and consistent success rate. And yes, here again, it's a trade-off between high principles and sustainable results. From my admittedly pragmatic angle of vision, it seems that if the Catholic Church could ever see its way clear to constraining the rights of the "potentially conceived" in favor of those *already conceived* (i.e., contraception as the only realistic "preferable alternative" to abortion), I suspect that the vast bulk of its pro-life agenda would be instantly achieved.

4. SAFEGUARDING LEGAL ACCESS

While abortion is never the preferred option, I believe it needs to remain *a protected legal option.* The Wisdom model provides additional validation for doing so in affirming the equal importance of all stages of life and exposing the implicit Catholic/evangelical theological bias at work in the presumption that the rights of the unborn take precedence over the rights of the mother. In an increasingly pluralistic America, where many religions and no religion offer competing moral compasses, it is more important than ever to establish a legally protected space in which difficult personal decisions can be arrived at through personal conscience, not through the legal imposition of sectarian dogma. I return here again to my earlier proposal of a "two-tier" system stipulating that included among the fundamental "first tier" rights is:

> *The right for a woman to control her own body and to hold the decisive vote as to whether a new life will be formed within her body.*

Beyond that baseline—at what I've called "second tier"—adherents of specific religious paths would have the full freedom to practice a higher level of moral observance according to the understandings of their particular faith tradition. It simply would not be universally binding.

5. CREATING A WIDER ETHICAL FORUM

Beyond those immediate issues raised by the abortion issue itself, the even greater challenge has proved to lie in figuring out a way to hold this conversation at all! And I'm not just talking about the differences of opinion and occasionally painful give-and-take as challenging new ideas are collectively pondered; I'm asking why thoughtful pondering of the kind we've been sharing here is such a painful rarity in our cultural conversation nowadays. As I racked my brain to think of a journal, a publishing house, an academic or retreat setting that might sponsor such a discussion, I quickly realized there were none. "Too far afield" for traditional theological journals; "too political" for academic or contemplative specializations; "too provocative" for retreat or even Living School fare, where one wishes to avoid giving offense to those who might be challenged or made personally uncomfortable by the exchange—"Cynthia is misusing her post as a teacher to wander into such dangerous personal ground."

It has seemed to me for a long time now that the most urgent long-range need facing our country today is for some cultural forum—beyond an internet blog series—where the important questions and issues impinging on our common humanity can actually be weighed and discussed. A Wisdom chautauqua, as it were. But what sort of forum would that be, and where would it take place?

Traditionally issues of ethics and morality have been discussed and enforced within specific faith traditions. But today there is no longer a single faith tradition undergirding our civic morality, and given the prevailing contemporary interpretation of the First Amendment, it is no longer easily acceptable to teach subject matter traditionally identified as belonging to the "religious" sector in a secular educational setting. The big questions that have traditionally guided human ethical progress—"*Who am I?*" "*What am I here for?*" "*Who is my neighbor?*" "*Is there anything beyond self-interest?*" "*Is there a higher purpose or coherence to the universe?*"—are perceived as spiritually booby-trapped (alas, often true!) and hence off-limits for the purposes of public education. Meanwhile, given the continuing hemorrhaging in most mainstream religious denominations, it is far from a foregone conclusion that younger generations of Americans will be exposed to these ideas even within a religious setting.

The vacuum is lethal—filled, by default, simply with the clichés and role-modeling available from the entertainment and marketing sectors. The highest and finest of what has traditionally made us human has effectively been closed out of our cultural transmission.

This becomes particularly pressing when we attempt to explore the concept of a developmental soul, for it clearly presumes *a sacred context* for the human condition, a meaning to life not realized in personal self-maximization but in cosmic obligation and the sense of participation in a larger coherent whole. It is here and only here, the great sacred traditions unanimously affirm, that the ultimate meaning and satisfaction of human life are to be found. It is here and only here, one might add, that the attitudes, vision, and practices that can carry our planet safely into the future are to be found. And it is only at this scale—against the wider backdrop of the meaning of *all* of life, considered as a unified transcosmic whole, will the meaning and gravity of fetal abortion finally come into a rightful perspective.

If we are not able even to raise these questions—let alone, wrestle with them, grow into them—what hope do we have in steering our planet wisely through these turbulent times?

Like many citizens in our country today, I've come to hate gerrymandering—that political sleight of hand that hacks up functional geopolitical units in order to create political firewalls. But even more than political gerrymandering, I loathe cultural and spiritual gerrymandering, which chops up the unified terrain of the human heart into a thousand-fold denominational and academic fiefdoms in such a way that the great river of our collective human wisdom can no longer flow freely through it. The tragedy, of course, is that it is only our collective human wisdom that will save us.

Any bright ideas as to how such a container might be created?

September 17, 2017
Northeast Wisdom at northeastwisdom.org

1. *Black's Law Dictionary defines "murder" as the unlawful killing of a human being by another with malice aforethought, either expressed or implied. A "homicide" is defined as the act of a human being in taking away the life of another human being.*

CHRISTIAN NONDUALITY–
SERIOUSLY??

The first time I ever recall hearing the word "nondual" was back in the early 1990s, after I'd uprooted my career as an Episcopal parish priest and headed west to join the circle of interspiritual seekers forming around Fr. Thomas Keating in Snowmass, Colorado. In the vibrant East/West exchange he called into being through his personal fascination with nondual realization, I began to learn a whole new vocabulary and a whole new roadmap.

Up until then, as a traditionally trained Christian spiritual teacher, my horizons had been entirely framed within the "purgative/illuminative/unitive" roadmap that has guided Christian spiritual progress for nearly fifteen hundred years. (Roughly speaking, *purgative* describes a preliminary phase of purification; *illuminative* describes a soul functioning in high attunement with the divine but still retaining a sepa-

rate sense of selfhood; *unitive* points toward a mysterious further melding of wills and spirits into a single tapestry of divine love.) Faced with a decidedly
apples–and–oranges comparison (the Eastern maps
featuring levels of consciousness; the Western de-
grees of affective union), it took quite a bit of
scrambling to discover what the closest point of
equivalency might be.

I was not the only one scrambling, it turned out.
Although the term "non-dual" has become decided-
ly trendy in Christian contemplative circles nowa-
days, definitions of what the term actually means
tend to be all over the map. Is "nondual" simply the
Eastern term for prolonged mystical experience?
The functional equivalent of "unitive" on the old
roadmap? The suspension of polarized thinking?
The suspension of *all* thinking? All of the above?
None of the above?

Meanwhile, there are still plenty of naysayers out
there who insist that Christianity has *no* nondual tradition, *period*, because of its stubborn affection for
theistic language and dualistic theology. If God is "a
Being" "out there," to be adored and anthropomor-
phized, is that not a telltale sign of a religion still
operating at a lower level of consciousness?

Yes, point ceded: it's true that the language in
which much of Christian mystical discourse is
couched is heavily, sometimes even blatantly, affective and erotic. You have to read between the lines

to see what's really at stake.

But I think it's worth reading between the lines. Because what's at stake is a very rich bank of insights. And part of what I'm up to in my latest book, *The Heart of Centering Prayer: Nondual Christianity in Theory and Practice* is to try to show you how to read between the lines.

The first and most important suggestion I make here is that the closest Christian equivalent to the term "non-dual" is not "unitive," but rather, the term *contemplation*—or at least contemplation as it was originally understood.

One of the less than fortunate side effects of the contemplative reawakening spurred by Thomas Keating and others has been an unintentional devaluing of the original scope and depth of the meaning of the term itself. With the proximate goal of getting Christians *en masse* back onto the meditation mats, modern reconstructions have tended to spin contemplation as the *emptying* of all content in favor of a pure "resting in God" somewhat akin to Eastern states of *sunnyata*. But this is quite a modern oversimplification! In the original tradition (i.e., the Patristic fathers of the early Christian centuries) contemplation was far from content-free; it's simply that the content was not generated or processed through the normal channels of the "faculties" (the reason, emotion, memory, will), but instead reflect some higher bandwidth of perceptivity entirely beyond the reaches of the usual functioning of the mind. Contemplation as originally understood invoked a higher, luminous knowledge, a "knowledge impregnated by love," in the famous sixth century description of St. Gregory the Great.

As my book demonstrates, this does not mean a rapturous mystical experience; it is rather a kind of coded language for describing a peculiar kind of attention—sometimes called "*vigilance*," "*recollection*," or "*attention of the heart*"—which in turn undergirds a whole new mode of perception—a whole new operating system, as it were.

What's more, I show how this other operating system (if we can think of it this way) is not merely an extension of the cognitive line, as it tends to be depicted on modern maps of levels of consciousness such as those emerging from Spiral Dynamics or Ken Wilber's Integral Theory. Christian mystical tradition is unanimous that this quantum leap to what Wilber calls "third tier" consciousness is not merely a matter of *what* one sees, but *how* one sees; it rests on an anatomical rewiring that literally features "putting the mind in the heart." While this veritable mantra of the Eastern Orthodox hesychastic tradition might be misconstrued as merely advocating emotion over thinking, it is very clear from the texts themselves that "putting the mind in the heart" is not merely a devotional attitude; it is accompanied by specific instructions on concentrating and holding attention in the region of the chest, effecting what contemporary neuroscience would more typically describe as an entraining of the brainwaves to the rhythms of the heart. Attention of the heart is not merely a metaphor; it denotes a whole new *physiology of perception* without which permanent nondual attainment is impossible.

This insight is for me the singular and most compelling contribution of the West to our contemporary conversation on nonduality. And note that I am broadening the field here intentionally, for the core insight originally articulated by Jesus in— "blessed are the pure in heart for they shall see God"—certainly radiated in all directions throughout the Near East, finding its home not only in the patristic fathers and Eastern Orthodoxy, but later and quintessentially in Sufism, whose teachings on the heart as an organ of spiritual perception have in my opinion never been surpassed.

But it's also possible to trace the lineaments of this nondual lineage even in the Christian West, hidden right there in plain sight. Armed with the clues that 1) contemplation really designates a level of consciousness, not a mystical experience, and 2) "love" refers not so much to an emotion as to the sensate experience of perception grounded in the heart, I set out in Part III of my book to explore the nondual teaching implicit in that fourteenth century spiritual classic, *The Cloud of Unknowing*. While the

142

work is generally classified as a specimen of monastic "love mysticism"—again, principally because of its celebrated line that:

God can be glimpsed and held fast by love, but by means of thought, never—

I believe it is actually a pioneering study in the phenomenology of consciousness, with "thought" signaling mental reflection (what Wilber would call the *rational* level) and love signaling that deeper, integral bandwidth when the mind is gathered in the heart. For the author of *The Cloud*, the "work" of contemplation—as he explicitly describes it—is to learn patiently to restrain the attention from its tendency to stream outward and attach itself to objects and learn instead how to hold attentiveness in a diffuse, objectless awareness which he picturesquely describes as "the cloud of unknowing." With the attention thus gathered, a deeper kind of knowingness emerges which is indeed, as Gregory the Great would have it, "knowledge impregnated with love."

In Christianity, as in all sacred traditions, the levels of realized practice encompass a wide bandwidth, ranging on one end to superstition and tribalism and at the other to a luminous window into the infinite. My hope in *The Heart of Centering Prayer* has been to create some handholds through which those two "apples–and–oranges" visions of the spiritual journey can come into meaningful dialogue, and through which the lineaments of nondual realization weaving through the entire Christian tradition can be better called out and celebrated. For the view is actually terrific.

~November 2017
Winter 2017 Mind Body Spirit, Watkins #52

"WHAT ENNEAGRAM TYPE
IS CYNTHIA?"

For almost thirty years the standing joke has been
"What enneagram type is Cynthia?" Leading teachers in all the various schools have typed me variously (frequently *categorically*) as a Four, Five, or Six.
While I can see certain points of congruence (after
all, my Mom was a Four, my Dad a Six, and most of
my partners Fives, so I know these types well), none
of them really resonated—and more important,
none of them really captured my interest. They
failed to paint for me any authentic description of
where I was pinned, or the road to authentic freedom—more authentic, at least, than what I already
knew in my own heart of hearts. And thus, I simply
lost interest in the entire psychometric. When people ask me my type nowadays, I usually just smile
and say, "I'm a ten."

On my very first encounter with this system
nearly thirty years ago—through Helen Palmer's
book, *The Enneagram*—I initially self-identified as a

Seven. The story starts out right: perceived lack of parental nurturance, *Puer Aeternus* (eternal youth), planning (gottcha!) But the narrative runs off the rails when it comes to the core passion (gluttony) and the reason behind it: self-distraction from pain, the need to maintain a cheery, spontaneous, excitement and adventure-laden dance card. This simply never resonated; it still doesn't (either I am totally un-self-aware or else the person who invented the Seven story was clearly not a Seven). And so again and again I would approach the Seven story as intrinsically energetically congruent, only to be thrown back by the mountain of narrative evidence arguing against it.

I would add that in the various tests I've taken online (RHETI and otherwise), the Seven doesn't usually come up as a strong contender. That's because the choice points presented for discernment always feature "pleasure," "excitement," "fun-loving," "spontaneous." When these are set against responsibility, goal-orientedness, concern for others, capacity to face pain, and willingness to make and keep long term commitments, I always wind up getting parceled out among more dutiful types. As for the celebrated enneagram panels—forget them! All players know their scripts and simply arrange the evidence, and even their voice tone to confirm their prior self-identifications…

But what if the Seven type were to prioritize restlessness, compulsive motion, fear of constriction, underlying existential anxiety? What then? When I asked Helen Palmer if there was any possibility that the type narrative was inaccurate or incomplete, she responded that that pretty much clenched the case that I was a Four (need to be a special case).

Anyway, thirty years later—and spurred into action by a review copy of Christopher Heuerts's new book, *The Sacred Enneagram*, which I found insightful but still basically recycling the old typologies—I am finally getting around to taking that risk. If in trying to elucidate the deeper waters of the Seven I prove myself indubitably a Four, so be it. But I think there is something here that is still not being seen by enneagram aficionados, and if these deeper waters were better understood, a lot of people like myself who still find themselves without a home base in the enneagram might find a way in.

This is a first gambit, but see what you think. Over the course of the summer I've shared it privately with several of my enneagram colleagues including Richard Rohr, Russ Hudson, Jeanine Siler-Jones, and Leslie Hershberger, and their comments have been enormously helpful as I continue to fine-tune my observations.

So now, for all of you out there: In your experience, do you know any Sevens that work the way I'm laying out here? I'm mostly interested in whether you think there's enough merit in what I'm suggesting here to warrant a more comprehensive re-evaluation of this particular personality type...

By the way, if my typology here is correct, I think there's absolutely no doubt that Teilhard de Chardin was a Seven. Maybe that's why he keeps pulling me in...

Anyway, here's my report, with a couple of short personal vignettes at the end to flesh things out. And yeah, after all these years, I'm finally claiming Seven as my home plate.

ENNEAGRAM TYPE SEVEN (BOURGEAULT REVISION)

HOLY IDEA...*Freedom*
VIRTUE...*Presence*
BASIC FEAR...*Annihilation*
BASIC DESIRE...*Fullness of Being*
FIXATION...*Planning*
PASSION...*Accidie (existential restlessness, "the noonday demon")*

As children, Sevens felt *trapped*, subject to the authority of caregivers who seemed unresponsive or even inexplicably hostile to their deepest being needs. While from the outside the nurturance received during their childhood may have appeared stable and conventional, from the inside it registered as hollow, frequently duplicitous, and sometimes downright treacherous. An underlying sense of *disconnection*—between call and response, appearance and reality—became the filter through which the Seven learned to view the world, leading to a chronic (and at times acute) sense of existential dread.

Resilient and inherently life-loving and optimistic, Sevens learned early on to become skilled self-nurturers—but always with that signature Seven wound: a restless addiction to forward motion and hyper-vigilance against any form of *confinement* that would appear to limit their options, cut off their escape routes, or impinge upon their ability to "help themselves." Sevens need to "feel the wind whistling in their ears" to outrun a pervasive sense of existential dread and emptiness, an inability to rest comfortably in their own skins.

THE CORE PASSION

The passion classically assigned to the Seven is *gluttony*, but I believe this assignation rests on a misunderstanding of the true motivation driving the Seven typology, plus a comparable misunderstanding of the true nature of the passion in question. The correct match-up is actually *accidie*, typically but incorrectly understood as *sloth* (and hence assigned to the Nine). Famously characterized by the early desert fathers as "the noonday demon," *accidie* is not primarily sloth (i.e., passivity or sluggishness), but the sense of *paralyzing dread* called forth by the engulfing immediacy of the present, where the egoic escape route of "flight into the future" is cut off and one is face to face with the inescapable reality of the *Now*. It is against this noonday demon that Evagrius issued his counsel, "Sit in your cell and it will teach you everything." But it is exactly this sitting in your cell that is so terrifying to the Seven, for it means sitting in that primal place of annihilation, where the child's desperate cries for succor went unheard.

For many Sevens, the profile of gluttony may indeed appear to fit—superficially, at least. Some do indeed wind up piling up a lifetime full of high living and endless exciting adventures. But the real driving motivation, I believe, is never the self-nurturing itself, *but maintaining the freedom-of-motion which the Seven believes is required in order to perform these self-nurturing rituals.* In the midst of a banquet, the Seven will already be mentally orchestrating the next banquet; what is missing is not the nurturance but the *Now*. The hollowness and emptiness of that primordial experience of non-nurturance continues to replay itself endlessly as the Seven reaches for the stars— and comes up with only a hand full of stardust.

Sevens hide in time. It is in the relentless planning, orchestrating, designing, creating options and possibilities, that the Prospero's castle that passes for their life is constructed and maintained. To deconstruct it appears to them like sure and certain death. But unfortunately, the fullness of Being that they so desperately seek can only be found in the Now. This is their great spiritual challenge.

The real pathology is not "distraction from their pain" and dissipation, as the classic Enneagram Seven story reads. Most Sevens I know are actually intensely focused and have high levels of tolerance for personal pain and the painful inner scrutiny to be paid for self-knowledge. The core pathology is not distraction but *flight*. Cessation of motion—i.e., stillness—feels like death to them, and they are too adept, too wary, to die in an ambush, even by Infinite Love.

TRANSFORMATION FOR THE SEVEN
THE HOLY IDEA AND VIRTUE

"Sit in your cell and it will teach you everything." This is indeed the terrifying eye of the needle the Seven will have to thread to move from "*choice freedom*" (as both Thomas Merton and Beatrice Bruteau call it)—i.e., freedom experienced as "keeping my options open," to "*spontaneity freedom*:" freedom experienced as the capacity to say "yes" wholeheartedly to *Now*; freedom to trust the primordial nurturance to be found only in the plenitude of presence. In such a way, and only in such a way, does the Seven finally come to rest—and in the simple immediacy of the presence there find, as St. Augustine (probably himself a Seven) so profoundly summarized: "Our hearts are restless until they rest in God."

TWO PERSONAL VIGNETTES TO ILLUSTRATE THE ABOVE POINTS

TRAPPED!!

At the age of seven months I suffered a nearly fatal bout with pneumonia at the hands of my Christian Science mother, who refused on religious principle to call a doctor. When the doctor was finally summoned, at the insistence of my grandmother (herself a Christian Science practitioner), he examined me gravely and concluded that I was beyond help. "But you were simply too stubborn to die," my Father recalls, as breath by breath I fought my way back to life.

I have no direct memory of this incident, of course. But the trauma still lives on in my body in a nervous swallow and residual anxiety around breathing. And even before I could think or speak, I already knew as a core datum of my life that my

152

mother could not be counted on as my protector; I would have to "help myself."

HIDING IN TIME

When I was three years old, I was formally enrolled in Christian Science Sunday school. The preschool class was intentionally located a bit out of earshot of the other groups, and after opening exercises, our small group of toddlers was led by the teacher up a narrow stairway to a tiny, closet-like classroom at the end of the hall. I panicked. Where were they taking me? Would I ever be released? I screamed in terror for my parents, but my cries elicited no response—neither from my parents (who were actually right on the other side of the classroom wall), nor from the teacher, who simply informed me that the longer I misbehaved, the longer it would take for the class to be over.

As I tried desperately to avoid a total meltdown, my attention fell on something that looked like a big dinner plate hanging on the wall, with numbers painted around the edge and two hands that moved in what seemed like a slow but regular way. And as I began to pay attention to this strange object over the next few weeks, I began to notice that when the big hand moved around the dial to the

153

place where it pointed directly at the ceiling, then the teacher offered a closing prayer and we were led back downstairs.

So that was it! No more panic helplessness. I'd learned that all I had to do was to wait till the big hand pointed straight up at the ceiling, and my release would be assured. I'd learned the secret of their game, and knew that I could count on it to protect me.

Thus began my addiction to "tempus fugit" as a surrogate form of nurturance and an escape route from the existential terror I by this time knew only too well.

~November 20, 2017
Northeast Wisdom at northeastwisdom.org

"GATE, GATE, PARAGATE
PARASAMAGATE…"

("GONE, GONE, GONE BEYOND,
GONE UTTERLY BEYOND…")

IS SACRED REALITY REALLY REAL?

*We used to chant this ancient Hindu Chant in
our small contemplative circle in Snowmass, Colorado, back in the early 1990s, during the
"Advaita" phase of our work. I hadn't thought of
it for years, but it suddenly popped back into my
mind this morning as the following exchange with
a student flowed out of me, from where I do not
know. I think I may actually have just encapsulat-
ed in about 800 words everything I really wanted
to say in my next book, currently (and a little too
Sisyphus-fully) on the drawing boards. Anyway,
for what it's worth… Happy formlessness…*

THE QUESTION...

Dear Cynthia,

I have very much appreciated your teachings and approach to the spiritual life. I'm writing because I've been increasingly bothered for the last several months with the doubt that there is an actual spiritual, supernatural realm beyond our human experience. I truly believe we human beings have deep spiritual experience, even a mystical sense of union with God. But how can we know that this experience is connected to anything real beyond the perceptions of our brains? I just have this nagging doubt that once our brains die, everything goes dark. It makes less and less sense to me how we could retain, or regain, consciousness and personhood after death as the doctrine of the resurrection promises.

These questions have become an obstacle to my prayer. I feel like I need to know (or have better-understood intellectual reasons for wagering) that there is an objectively real spiritual realm beyond earth and the human brain, in order to pray with motivation and hope.

Could you let me know how you know? Or the reasons you come back to for trusting in the reality of a spiritual realm that transcends the experiences (however profound) of our bodies and minds?

AND MY RESPONSE...

Thank you for sharing with me this profound and delicate transition point in your own journey. Both the clarity and the honesty with which you reveal your struggle suggest you're really standing at the edge of a major paradigm shift. I'd almost be inclined to say the one that ushers you through the gate into the authentic nondual.

It's clear that your old cosmology of God—and the prayers emerging from it—is crumbling before your eyes, and that's good. But what replaces it?

One way to go, certainly, is to simply replace your previous theological/metaphysical castle with a new one, generated by the same mechanisms of the brain, only this time more spacious. The whole metaphysical postulation of a supernatural or "imaginal" realm speaks directly to that strategy.

Throughout the spiritual ages, across all the sacred traditions, there has been a cloud of witnesses who can validate that personhood beyond the physical realm does indeed exist. I have had the perhaps questionable privilege of being able to travel in this realm a bit over these past twenty years on the eagle's wings of my spiritual teacher Rafe. So I know that there is indeed water in this well, and that the well does indeed water the earth and materially help it through the recurring drought times and deserts of the human spirit. Yet I know also that even this well ultimately proves to be a construction. Just as everything in this all-too-perishable realm ultimately reveals itself to be.

But this doesn't mean it's false—only impermanent, as the Buddhists would say. In his recent book *Waking, Dreaming, Being*, philosopher Evan Thompson has a brilliant one-liner: "All illusions are constructions, but not all constructions are illusions." The impermanent, intermediate, and ultimately mirage-like nature of the surrounding imaginal/supernatural world is indeed a construction. But so is the cosmos itself (and the word "cosmos" in Greek means "ornament"): a beautiful, construction through which the otherwise inaccessible white light of the divine heart becomes manifest. We all participate in that illusion, each to our own degree, to our own level of clarity and toughmindedness. And good is done here—as well as some measure of harm. In the words of the old Koranic maxim, God speaks and says, "I was a hidden treasure and I longed to be known, so I created the worlds, visible and invisible." All of us, in our temporarily separated individual conscious viewing platforms are pixels participating in that grand construction, the revelation of the divine heart. It is all fiction. And it is all real.

But another way of moving through this impasse—and the way I think you're actually intuiting here—is not to build another cosmic Prospero's castle using the same old mental methodology, but to *question the nature of the mind itself* in its seemingly unbreakable addiction to mentally constructed meaning. What would it mean to live "bare," without that whole mental castle?

A scary threshold, to be sure. Few reach it, and the few who do generally get scared shitless and go running back as quickly as possible to the world of constructed meaning. But it *is* possible to stand there and to stand well. Beyond the cloud of constructed meaning, there *is* such a thing as direct perception. And you can get there if you wish—if you can stand it.

As Thomas Merton observed, shortly before the close of his life, in his own devastating moment of final clairvoyance (which I can almost but not quite quote from memory): "I was jerked out of my habitual, half-tied way of looking at things…having seen through every question without trying to discredit anyone or anything—without refutation, without establishing some other argument." The constructive principle drops out, and what remains is simply bare seeing.

And it's just here that one discovers the remarkable, elusive secret: that *meaning and explanation are not the same thing.* Explanation is of the mind. Meaning is of the heart, a felt-sense of belongingness that needs neither justification nor further action. It is simply its own fullness. Prayer does not reach it, for it is the *source* of prayer, the source of everything.

Rest assured that consciousness does not go dark when your individual pixel of it departs from its individual body container. The only thing that goes dark—that is to say, if you decide to forego a side trip through the imaginal or boddhisattva bardos and proceed directly to the heart of the infinite—is your individual *relationship* to consciousness. Consciousness is the stuff of the universe, undivided and whole. It will never go dark. It will simply enfold "you," and the exile will be over…

I'm not sure this helps; but hopefully it at least affirms that you're standing on sacred ground, and that cynicism is not the only option. The other is to deepen the wonder.

Blessings, Cynthia

January 28, 2018
Northeast Wisdom at northeastwisdom.org

"WHUR WE COME FROM..."

"Teachers of contemplative Christianity, who acknowledged the limitations of human knowledge and the inconstant nature of human sentiment, instead encouraged a commitment to practice. A scripturally grounded commitment to practice and service—rather than a reliance on unsteady belief and feeling—is the fulcrum of contemplative Christianity."

~ *Paula Pryce, The Monk's Cell*

From time to time in the unfolding life of a lineage, it becomes important to stop and ponder together "Whur we come from" (as my teacher Rafe used to call it): i.e., the fundamental understandings that called us into being as a particular expression of the wider tradition of Christian contemplative Wisdom. As the Contemplative Society, our flagship Wisdom vessel (which you may find at contemplative.org), now celebrates its twentieth anniversary and a new

161

generation of seekers and board members assume their turn at the helm, it seems like an appropriate occasion for just such a moment of reflection.

Wisdom, like water, is itself clear and formless, but it necessarily assumes the shape and coloration of the container in which it is captured. Between formless essence and manifesting particularity there is a reciprocal dynamism; you can't have one without the other.

Our own particular branch of the great underground river of Wisdom came to the surface about twenty years ago, flowing within two major riverbanks: a) the Christian mystical tradition of *theosis*–divinization—particularly as lived into being in the Benedictine monastic tradition, and b) the practical training in mindfulness and non-identification as set forth in the Gurdjieff Work. The fusion of these two elements was the original accomplishment of my spiritual teacher Br. Raphael Robin, who formed me in this path and just before his death in 1995 sent me off to Canada to teach it. It is a distinct lineage within the wider phylum of *sophia perennis*—perennial Wisdom—and as with all particular containers, it has its own integrity and its own heart.

Here, then, is my own quick shortlist of the eight main elements—or defining characteristics—for our particular branch of this Wisdom verticil:

1. We are founded on a daily practice of sitting meditation, predominantly but not exclusively Centering Prayer, anchored within the overall daily rhythm of "ora et labora," as set forth in the Rule of St. Benedict.

2. We are rooted in the Christian mystical and visionary tradition, understanding contemplation in its original sense as "luminous seeing," not merely a meditation practice or a lifestyle. In service to this luminous seeing, we affirm the primacy of the language of silence and its life-giving connection with the subtle realms, without which spiritual inquiry tends to become overly cognitive and contentious.

3. We incorporate a major emphasis (much more so than in more conventional contemplative circles) on mindfulness and conscious awakening, informed here particularly by the inner teachings of G.I Gurdjieff and by their parallels and antecedents in the great sacred traditions, particularly in Sufism.

4. We are an esoteric or "gnostic" school to the extent that these terms have come to be understood as designating that stream of Christian transmission through which the radically consciousness-transforming teachings of Jesus have been most powerfully transmitted and engaged. But we eschew esotericism as simply mental or metaphysical speculation, and we affirm the primacy of the scripture and tradition as the cornerstones of Christian life.

5. Also in contrast to many branches of the Wisdom tradition based on Perennial or Traditionalist metaphysics (with its inherently binary and anti-material slant), we are emphatically a Teilhardian, Trinitarian lineage, embracing asymmetry (three-ness), evolution, and incarnation in all their material fullness and messiness.

6 We are moving steadily in the direction of revisioning contemplation no longer in terms of monastic, otherworldly models prioritizing silence and repose, but rather, as a way of honing consciousness and compassion so as to be able to fully engage the world and become active participants in its transition to the higher collectivity, the next evolutionary unfolding.

7. We are an integral school, not a pluralistic one, (to draw on Ken Wilber's levels of consciousness); our primary mission field is teal, not green. Our work concentrates not at the level of healing the false self, woundedness and recovery, substance abuse, equal rights, restorative justice or political correctness (although we acknowledge the importance of all of these initiatives), but rather at the level of guiding the transition from identity based primarily in the narrative or egoic self to identity stabilized at the level of witnessing presence, or "permeably boundaried" selfhood.

8. Our most important teachers and teachings are Jesus, St. Benedict, The Canonical and Wisdom gospels; The Cloud of Unknowing, *the greater Christian mystical and visionary tradition (including Eckhart, Boehme, Thomas Merton, Thomas Keating, Ladislaus Boros, Bernadette Roberts), the Desert and Hesychastic traditions; Bede Griffiths and the Christian Advaitic traditions (including Raimon Panikkar, Henri LeSaux/Abishiktananda and Bruno Barnhart); Rumi, Sufism, G.I. Gurdjieff, Pierre Teilhard de Chardin. And of course my own teacher, Br. Raphael Robin.*

Please know that this list is intended to start a conversation, not end it. In the upcoming months, I hope to unpack each of these points more fully. I invite others in our Wisdom network to do likewise, both in your larger organizations (The Contemplative Society, Northeast Wisdom, Wisdom Southwest, Wisdom Way of Knowing, etc.) and in your smaller practice circles. Collectively, let's see if we can discover about our lineage, as we midwifed it through a first generation and now transmit through a second.

Blessings, Cynthia

February 26, 2018
Northeast Wisdom at northeastwisdom.org.

ABOUT CYNTHIA

The Reverend Cynthia Bourgeault, Ph.D., is an Episcopal priest who lives on the North Atlantic coast in Stonington, Maine. Her time is spent between solitude on her island hermitage and traveling around the world in her role as writer, speaker, teacher and leader of retreats.

Cynthia grew up in Pennsylvania, outside the city of Philadelphia. There, where Amish country begins, the natural world was at her fingertips. Her mother was a devout Christian Scientist, with its strict emphasis on a spiritual reality and illusory material world. As a young girl Cynthia attended a Quaker school, deeply resonating with the quiet freedom of Quaker Meeting. As a young person growing up in the 1950's, the force of her Christian Scientist upbringing, the ready access to the divine in nature and the intimacy she found in the silence all provided maps to wrestle with, and presence to discover. Cynthia later described these as "presence traditions", and relates how at 10 years old, schooled as she was in the direct immersion of silence and the immediacy of mystical religion, she experienced an opening while singing the verses of a hymn, suddenly sensing herself within a planetary oneness.

In high school Cynthia was inspired by a religion teacher who created an environment where the deep spiritual questions of life and religious thought were brought forth and opened up. She was also to meet her husband, a music teacher and father of her two daughters, in those early years. Her love of music has been a major thread throughout her life, marked at 25 when she received her Ph.D. in medieval studies and musicology.

Cynthia relates in her book *Wisdom Way of Knowing*, that two events prior to her Ph.D. had resonated deeply in her soul. The first, at eighteen, was her first encounter with Chartres Cathedral. Walking in, she was "completely magnetized" and felt both "relief and a sense of direction" that was a balm for that pervading part of her that had always felt "alien"—"stranded and disoriented." The second took place at twenty, when Cynthia visited an Episcopal Church (in order to hear a choir sing) and received communion for the first time. The effect was riveting. She felt deeply met, and had a particular sense of wonder about the experience of a reality in the communion, and further, a knowing what she knew, without doubt.

For several years afterwards she found herself witnessing an inner conflict of old fears and disbelief as her feet walked her to church daily for the noon Eucharist. Years later, as an ordained priest, she found herself drawn to the mystical and the monastic, questioning why Christianity so often seemed to miss the mark in practice, especially when it came to the centrality of its message of human consciousness, awake and alive in love; in this world, in this moment, in divine love and presence. A confluence of threads was at work in her particular biography and her awakening heart and heartbreak.

These questions led her to Bruno Barnhart, Father Thomas Keating and Beatrice Bruteau, among others. She first heard about centering prayer at New Camaldoli Monastery in Big Sur, California, where she became an oblate and came to call Bruno Barnhart a spiritual father and mother. The particular way that he appreciated and embodied the teachings of the East while remaining wedded to Christianity, and his dear friends Bede Griffiths and Raimon Panikkar, continued to open her own Christian ground of being. Later she traveled to Snowmass to train with Father Keating in centering prayer, and began teaching. In centering prayer she found a personal practice that has continued for decades, along with chanting the psalms, and the tenets of *The Benedictine Rule*, which she witnessed in action, working the souls of many in the monasteries she frequented.

Her questions took her as well to Jacob Needleman's classic 1980 book, *Lost Christianity*, where she was riveted by his treatment of the force of attention, and introduced for the first time to the Gurdjieff work. After working her way through the classic Fourth Way "starter book," P.D. Ouspensky's *In Search of The Miraculous*, she went in search of an actual Gurdjieff work group and eventually found her way to one in Nova Scotia. She commuted there for several years, studying, growing, and sensing her feet.

The ground that was being created through this weaving of encounters and practices in her life all came together in surprising ways, and bore fruit when she met Rafe, a hermit monk and the monastery mechanic at Snowmass. They soon discovered their common lineage; Rafe's daily practice included both scripture and *Psychological Commentaries*, the life work by Maurice Nicoll based on and inspired by his time with the Gurdjieff work.

The bond between Rafe and Cynthia is really unspeakable; a deep love lived between them that is best described in Cynthia's own words, which may be found in her first book, *Love is Stronger Than Death: The Mystical Union of Two Souls*, published first in 1999. By that time, beyond, and as part of, the path she walked with Rafe's tough love and beloved gaze, her influences included Jacob Boehme, Valentin Tomberg, JG Bennett, Boris Mouravieff, Helen

Luke, Ladislaus Boros's *The Mystery of Death*, Vladmir Solovyov, Thomas Merton, and Kabir Helminski, as well as the classic writings of John Donne, TS Eliot, Shakespeare, Rilke, *The Cloud of Unknowing*, and the Desert Fathers and Mothers including John Cassian.

After Rafe's death in 1995, five years after their meeting and the beginning of their intense sojourn together, Cynthia talks about "shaping her grief into a life's path of teaching and writing" (from a memorial piece she wrote for the Contemplative Society, "Remembering Bruno Barnhart," written in late 2015). In *Love is Stronger Than Death*, Cynthia speaks at length about their union, their continuing relationship after Rafe's death and the way Rafe spoke within her in mysterious ways that led her, with her trust, into a life she had no notion of.

Four years after Rafe died *Love is Stronger Than Death* was complete, and she had begun to facilitate and teach Wisdom tradition and practice. Centers of contemplative Wisdom work were developing in British Columbia and Aspen Colorado. These centers soon became The Contemplative Society and The Aspen Wisdom School, with Cynthia as founding director of both. Combining her wisdom gained through decades of Benedictine monastic practice with her deepening understanding of attention and mindfulness gained in her years in the Gurdjieff work, she offered her first Wisdom School on Salt Spring Island, British Columbia, in 1999. Within a decade, Wisdom Schools were operating on four continents.

Cynthia was the recipient of the 2014 Contemplative Voices award from Shalem Institute, and is a member of the GPIW (Global Peace Initiative for Women) Contemplative Council. Among numerous collaborations with contemporary spiritual teachers, she currently serves as core faculty with Richard Rohr and James Finley at the Center for Action and Contemplation in Albuquerque New Mexico, teaching in the Living School.

Cynthia's work continues to grow as she weaves the threads of her lineage with her experience in life into ever deeper expressions of the spiritual life as, ultimately, the living reality of transformation. Her particular offering speaks to the alchemy that engenders the potential to change life and perception—and that can assist to usher in a new paradigm of being—in order that, as persons, we may serve in the unique and specific way that each one of us took birth to.

~Laura Ruth
October 2017

ADDITIONAL BOOKS
AND RESOURCES
BY
CYNTHIA BOURGEAULT

Cynthia Bourgeault has been a prolific spiritual writer since 1999 when *Love is Stronger Than Death: The Mystical Union of Two Souls* was published.

On the heels of that first book came *Mystical Hope: Trusting in the Mercy of God* in 2001; *The Wisdom Way of Knowing* in 2003; *Centering Prayer and Inner Awakening* in 2004; and *Chanting the Psalms: A Practical Guide* in 2006.

In 2008, *The Wisdom Jesus; Transforming Heart and Mind—A New Perspective on Christ and His Message* was in print; followed by *The Meaning of Mary Magdalene: Discovering the Woman at the Heart of Christianity* in 2010; and *The Holy Trinity and The Law of Three* in 2013.

Her latest book is *The Heart of Centering Prayer: Non-dual Christianity in Theory and Practice*, published in 2016. Cynthia continues to write regularly and has two new books in the works.

In order to catch up on what is percolating for Cynthia, she posts regularly on these websites—all home to her—Northeast Wisdom, The Contemplative Society, Wisdom Way of Knowing and The Center for Action and Contemplation. Cynthia has been a contributing writer to journals, such as Parabola; Watkins; Kosmos and websites such as The Omega Center. Interviews are available through radio, such as Sounds True, and TV such as the UK based Conscious TV.

A number of audio books and teachings are available, that include Cynthia talks on the subjects of her books and retreats. Check out the websites mentioned above for more of these. Additionally, The Wisdom Way of Knowing, under Robbin Whittington's careful eye, has created Cynthia's first-ever online Introductory Wisdom School at wisdomwayofknowing.com. This will be followed by Part II: The Divine Exchange. Numerous online courses Cynthia has offered are currently available at The Center for Spirituality & Practice, and future courses are set to go; and her Four Voices of Discernment course is available at contemplativejournal.com.

A beautiful aspect of Cynthia's Wisdom lineage is that she continues to penetrate the experience and exploration of her Wisdom stream. Ever deepening and ever articulating the love, truth and beauty inherent within it—she responds to its lifeblood in the immediate—fearlessly and committedly. As a result, there is always new work on the horizon; with opportunities, alive and present, for those wanting and willing to dive in.

~Laura Ruth
January 2018

92602714R00116

Made in the USA
Middletown, DE
09 October 2018